A Comprehensive Study Guide On...

SPIRITUAL WARFARE PRAYER

**This guide teaches you how to
Pray in Authority Until the Answer Comes.**

MICKEY BONNER

Scripture quotations marked Amp. are taken from the Amplified Bible. Old Testament Copyright © 1965, 1987, by the Zondervan Corporation. New Testament Copyright © 1958, 1987, by the Lockman Foundation. Used by permission.

ISBN 1-878578-13-8
© By Mickey Bonner
All Rights Reserved
Published by Mickey Bonner Evangelistic Association
P.O. Box 680368, Houston, Texas 77268-0368
Printed in the United States of America

MICKEY BONNER EVANGELISTIC ASSOCIATION
P.O. Box 680368, Houston, Texas, 77268-0368
Phone: 281-444-7563, Fax: 281-580-0175

FOREWORD

Beloved Friends:

What you have before you is a composite work of many years of teaching in the area of Spiritual Warfare Prayer. I feel that this syllabus is a real weapon that can teach aggressive prayer in such a way that you will see not only changes in your own life, but in the lives of those for which you pray. This represents hundreds of hours of study and teaching world-wide. It can become one of the most powerful tools you have ever had in your hands, based on prayer.

This is not a manual _about_ prayer; it actually teaches you _how_ to pray in Authority until the answer comes. We have seen Churches take this teaching and explode with souls, depth, and change. Complete transformation occurs in the lives of Believers when they suddenly discover that God answers their personal prayers. That's the difference.

I urge you to study this Syllabus slowly. Look up every Scripture that is referenced, and then apply it actively and aggressively as you pray. From there you will be able to see God's Glory, not only to you, but through you. The events that satan uses to destroy will be changed in the lives of those for whom you are praying, resulting in victory.

It is the application of the Word of God that is _"sharper than any two-edged sword,"_ an instrument offensive in nature, aggressive in teaching, authoritative in doctrine, and life - changing in result. You are His weapon and He conducts His warfare through you. Again, I urge you to study this slowly, page by page applying its purpose. It works, or better said, He works through us, in answer to prayer.

This Syllabus is designed so that you as an individual can study, apply it, make it work, and then teach it. We have audio cassette tapes and videos that can be presented along with the Syllabus. It can be used as a study guide, with these other tools, or as a teaching tool by itself. However you use it, just use it, because Prayer works. Satan was defeated at the Cross by the Blood of Jesus. Please become familiar with Truth and experience the Power and Glory of God.

These are wonderful days! As the horizon of History darkens with the alienation of souls, we can stand with the Banner high. When prayer begins to work in your life, it will be as a light or beacon to the "Doxos" or "Glory" of God. Then, when you stand before God you will not be rewarded for what _you_ did in the Name of Jesus Christ, but what He was able to do _through_ you, as His servant.

How great our God! How wonderful His attributes! How wonderful He is to allow us to minister His grace in prayer. Get with it, remembering that the only evident sign of Spiritual maturity in the life of a Christian, is answered prayer. Grow and it will work, or better still, He works. Also remember there are all kinds of prayer. This study deals with one aspect: Warfare Praying.

God bless you. If you need more information or materials, please contact us.
In Christ,

Mickey Bonner

TABLE OF CONTENTS

SECTION ONE: **PRAYER IS BINDING SATAN** PAGE **3**

SECTION TWO: **ALL PRAYER IS WARFARE** PAGE **15**

SECTION THREE: **CONDUCTING WARFARE PRAYER** PAGE **25**

SECTION FOUR: **KNOW YOUR ENEMY: SATAN (4A)** PAGE **37**

        (4B) PAGE **41**

        (4C) PAGE **45**

SECTION FIVE: **5 U'S OF UNANSWERED PRAYER** PAGE **49**

SECTION SIX: **PRAYER: A WEAPON IN THE HANDS OF GOD** PAGE **65**

SECTION SEVEN: **PRAYER ASSAULT TEAMS** PAGE **73**

*(ALL SCRIPTURES USED IN THIS VOLUME ARE FROM THE KING JAMES VERSION UNLESS OTHERWISE DESIGNATED)

"PRAYER IS BINDING SATAN"

SECTION ONE

Beloved, as we move toward the 21st Century we will begin to see the most unbelievable things we will have ever witnessed, due to the open move of satanists in this nation as well as around the world, through the New Age and one-world government theme. The end times are truly being birthed before our eyes, (*Matt. 24*).

It is time to wake up, for the Games are over! The only thing that will hold back what is happening is God's hand moving into the matter as a result of answered prayer.

It is time that the Christians come alive in Christ, remembering that we won at the Cross. We Won!!!

All Prayer is Warfare!

Christ's ministry began with the Father, as does ours... *"Our Father which art in Heaven..."*

Q. What is Warfare?
A. Look at the Lord's Prayer for an example. *"Our Father which art in Heaven, Hallowed be Thy Name, Thy kingdom come, Thy will be done, on earth as it is in Heaven. Give us this day our daily bread, and forgive us our debts as we forgive our debtors. Lead us not into temptation but deliver us from the 'evil one'..."*

...Not just from "evil" as many references state, but from "poneros," the Greek word which means "the evil one," (*Amplified*).

So, when we pray we actually bring deliverance; for we are to bind satan in the lives of those for whom we are praying, *"...deliver us from the evil one..."*

God answers no prayers but His own.
"...Thy kingdom come, Thy will be done, on earth as it is in Heaven..." It must be understood that everyday of the Christian's life is already pre-planned or written out. "Religion" is trying to get God to join our plans. True Christianity is joining God's will through us in prayer.

For we are God's [own] handiwork (His workmanship), recreated in Christ Jesus, [born anew] that we may do those good works which God predestined (planned beforehand) for us, (taking paths which He prepared ahead of time) that we should walk in them - living the good life which He prearranged and made ready for us to live, (Ephesians 2:10 Amp.).

Therefore, the model prayer, (the Lord's Prayer) could be understood to mean, "Thy kingdom come, Thy will be done, on earth as it is written in heaven." We must join God's will for our lives.

I. Christ's Ministry Was That Of The Father Through Him.

A. The reason Christ came to this earth was to destroy the works of the devil, *(I John 3:8).* *"He that committeth sin is of the devil; for the devil sinneth from the beginning. For this purpose the Son of God was manifested, that he might destroy the works of the devil."*

Jesus did this by His...

1. Virgin Birth
2. Sinless life
3. Shedding of Blood for Atonement
4. Death, burial, and resurrection

To Understand the Working of Prayer You Must Realize that Jesus Never Worked a Miracle in His Life. His Entire Earthly Ministry was that of God's Power through Him.

B. Jesus never "worked" a miracle during his earthly ministry, *(John 5:17,19,30).*
17 But Jesus answered them, My Father worketh hitherto, and I work.
19 Then answered Jesus and said unto them, Verily, verily, I say unto you, The Son can do nothing of himself, but what he seeth the Father do: for what things soever he doeth, these also doeth the Son likewise.
30 I can of mine own self do nothing: as I hear, I judge: and my judgment is just; because I seek not mine own will, but the will of the Father which hath sent me.

Q. Who is speaking in *John 5:30?*
A. Jesus.

1. His ministry was the power of God through Him.
2. Jesus constantly separated Himself from others to pray and to seek the Will of the Father.

Prayer was the most important thing to Christ. For in His entire ministry, as these verses show, He could do nothing of Himself. It was the Father through Him.

Q. Who then was His source of Power?
A. God the Father.

John 5:19 Jesus states that as He prayed, He sought God's Will in every matter. As this was revealed to Him, He acted in faith and the miracles were performed.

Christ came to this earth to die, to become a human sacrifice for your sins. Therefore, He took on an earthly body, *"that He may become sin,"* *(II Cor. 5:21).*

C. Christ's Power was God through Him.

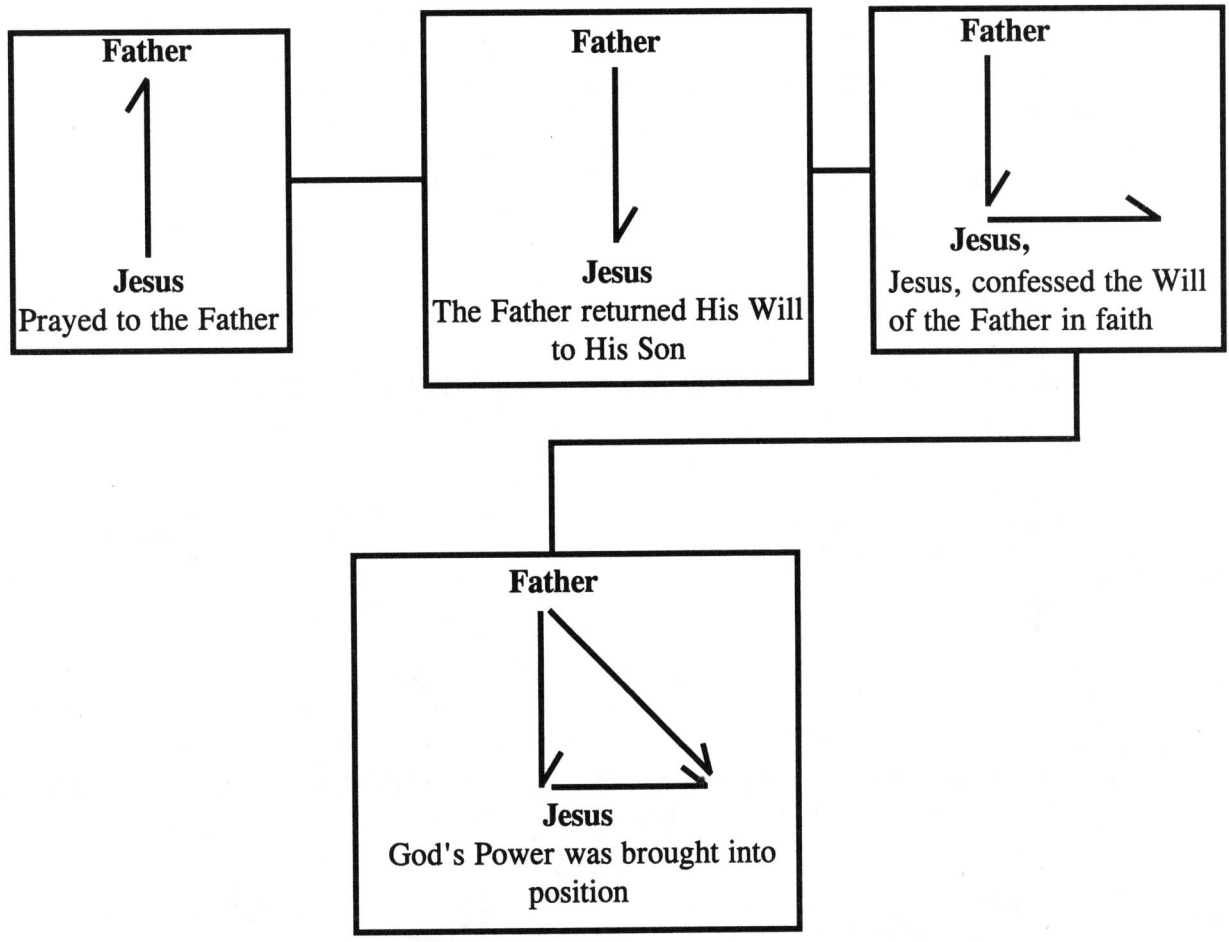

The above illustration explains how Christ's Power was displayed, that men might believe on Him.

The blind saw, the lame walked, the maimed were made whole, and the dead rose from the grave, by the Power of God through Christ in Prayer.

1. Jesus said in *John 5:19 "the Son is able to do nothing from Himself - of His own accord..." (Amp.)*

2. Christ's ministry was fulfilled totally by prayer. Prayer was more important to Him than sleeping and eating. He constantly sought to pray.

Christ never worked a miracle by His own accord. It was the Father through Him.

Therefore...

D. You must stop trying to live the Christian life (religion - law - works). Instead, let Jesus live His life through you.

Q. What was more important to Christ than sleep?
A. Prayer

Q. What did Christ constantly go apart and do?
A. Pray

Q. What does satan fight the most in the Christian's life?
A. Prayer

II. JESUS SAID HE COULD DO NOTHING OF HIMSELF. GOD IS THE POWER. (JOHN 5:30)

A. God enters into a matter through prayer, as the Christian is able in his spirit to hear God's Will and agree.

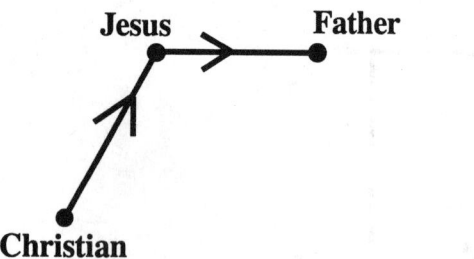

- Goes to God in the Name of Jesus Christ

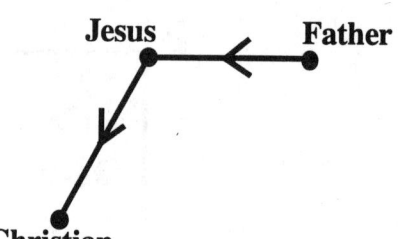

- The Father Comes back with His Will

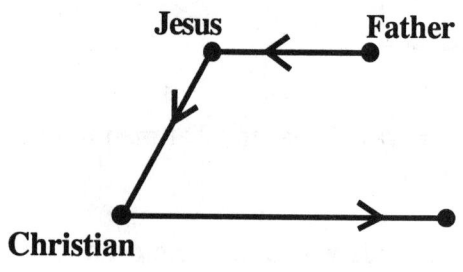

- Hears and agrees

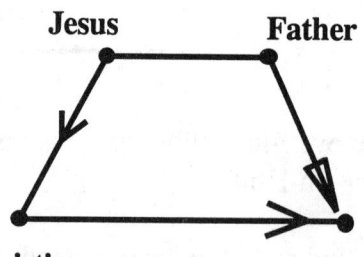

- God moves into the prayer by His Power

It is the same principle as when Christ was here on the earth. The Father ministered through Him. Now it is *"Christ in you, the hope of Glory."*

The major difference between Christ and you is the statement in *John 5:30 "...as I hear..."* Christ could hear because satan had nothing in Him to stop the voice and will of God, *(John 14:30)*.

Satan can cause strongholds in the lives of Christians, designed to keep them from hearing.

Example:

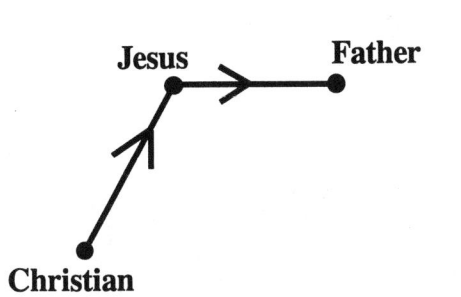

Christian
-Goes to God in the Name of Jesus Christ to receive His Will

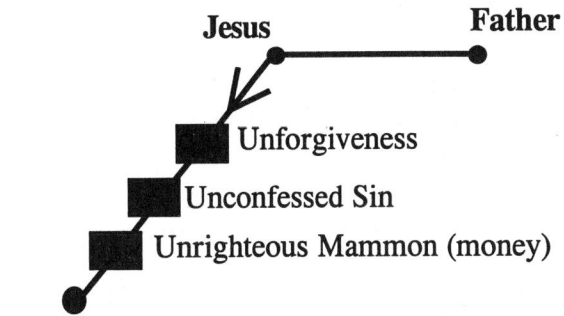

Unforgiveness

Unconfessed Sin

Unrighteous Mammon (money)

Christian
-God's Will cannot be heard because of hindrances to stop His Will. You must be able to hear the Will of God and agree, through the spirit's voice within your life.

B. The enemy fights against anything that even looks like active, aggressive prayer.
   1. In Churches
   2. In individuals
   3. In families

Recently, a major television talk show host interviewed a male witch. The question was asked, "What do you do?" The witch answered, "My life work is to destroy the Christian Church. I get into churches and become ordained as a deacon. Sometimes it takes as long as two and a half years. Once ordained, I make it my business to destroy the prayer base of the church. Once that is done I can walk off and leave it alone and it will never do anything again."

C. Everything, except prayer, can be counterfeited.
   1. Gifts
   2. Evangelism
   3. Teaching
   4. Christianity through religion

Prayer, through Christ, is God's power through man, *(I John 5:14-15).*

III. THE MINISTRY OF BINDING SATAN. (MATTHEW 12:22,23)

22 Then was brought unto him one possessed with a devil, blind, and dumb: and he healed him, insomuch that the blind and dumb both spake and saw.

23 And all the people were amazed, and said, Is not this the son of David?

24 But when the Pharisees heard [it], they said, This [fellow] doth not cast out devils, but by Beelzebub the prince of the devils.

Onlookers who knew Jesus religiously but not spiritually questioned His miracles, ("Is not this the son of David?" i.e., the kid who worked in his dad's carpentry shop).

A. When God begins to do a great work, corporately or individually, the first people who balk are the carnal or unsaved church members. This can include pastors or "religionists," those individuals who "academically" know or believe in God the Father, but do not personally know or believe from the heart.

B. The Pharisees, (religious leaders) actually ascribed to the devil the work of God's Holy Spirit, *(Matt. 12:24).* They declared that Jesus' power came from Beelzebub, (the lord of the flies).

C. Religious people refuse to believe in God's miracles if they do not occur in their particular group or denomination.
   1. There are over 20,000 groups or denominations.
   2. Many pastors do not believe in miracles.
   3. Hirelings (profiteers) discount His works.

D. It is satan's position to get people to ascribe God's true work as false, thereby discrediting the work, *(v.25-28).*

25 And Jesus knew their thoughts, and said unto them, Every kingdom divided against itself is brought to desolation; and every city or house divided against itself shall not stand:

26 And if Satan cast out Satan, he is divided against himself; how shall then his kingdom stand?

27 And if I by Beelzebub cast out devils, by whom do your children cast [them] out? therefore they shall be your judges.

28 But if I cast out devils by the Spirit of God, then the kingdom of God is come unto you.

Satan tries to discredit the true work of the Father by bringing confusion to the situation. Where there is confusion there is division. For example, a military unit that is under the specific orders from its superior, acts and functions as one, united. However, if that same military unit is cut off from its orders or superior, confusion sets in and division results, causing that military unit, which once acted as one, to be routed in battle.

Satan's work is to divide the home, the church, and families. He accomplishes this by getting people to look at each other's faults rather than walking together.

E. If you have unforgiveness against anyone, living or dead, saved or lost, God will not reveal His Will to you, *(II Cor. 2:10-11).*

> *10 To whom ye forgive any thing, I [forgive] also: for if I forgave anything, to whom I forgave [it], for your sakes [forgave I it] in the person of Christ;*
> *11 Lest Satan should get an advantage of us: for we are not ignorant of his devices.*

God commands you to forgive. The greek word for forgive is "carizomai," meaning "freely, totally, unconditionally." Unforgiveness in your life makes you ignorant. "Agnoeo," the Greek word for ignorant means "that which causes you to ignore God's position in the matter." What happens in this case is that satan stops your hearing God's Will by dividing you and God through anger or unforgiveness.

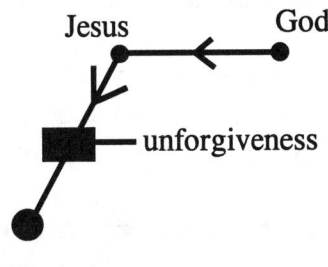

Christian

The Christian goes to God in the Name of Jesus. But His Will cannot return because the Christian walks in unforgiveness, thus blocking his hearing from God.

Satan gets the advantage over Christians by destroying their prayer life. Unforgiveness, (roots of bitterness), is his strongest weapon.

Simply put, if you have unforgiveness against anyone, living or dead, saved or lost, you cannot expect God to answer any of your prayers.

Q. What are you to do?
A. Forgive. Forgive the saved *(I John 2:7-12, 4:20)*, forgive the lost *(Matt. 6:14-15 Amp.)*

F. The only evident sign of maturity in the life of a Christian is answered prayer.
   1. The Kingdom of God is God's Will for your life, as pre-written in heaven, *(Matt. 6:9,33, Eph. 2:10 Amplified)*.
      To receive it you must assault it with violence, *(Matthew 11:12)*. Hunger, Thirst, Seek, Knock, Labor to enter into the rest. *"Thy Kingdom come,"* (God's plan for Christians,) *"Thy Will be done,"* (His work through them in answered prayer) *"on earth as it is in heaven,"* (God's plan being performed through the believers).
   2. Answered prayer is the only evidence that a believer is in right standing with God.
   3. The only thing you will be rewarded for at the Judgment seat, *(II Cor 5:10)*, is answered prayer - gold, silver, precious stones. Gold, silver, and precious stones are God's works through you. Wood, hay and stubble is your work in religion, *(I Cor. 3:12-15)*.

"Don't show me what you're doing for Jesus, show me what Jesus is doing through you."

G. In Warfare Praying, pray for one thing at a time, *(Luke 18:1 / section 2)*.
   1. Win one battle at a time.
   2. Don't start prayer for a second issue until you've received a peace or "release" from the first issue. Submit to God, resist the devil and he will flee from you, because of the Lord in you as a result of prayer.

(We will discuss this further in Section 2)

IV. PRAYER IS "...BINDING THE STRONGMAN." *(MATTHEW 12:29)*

"One cannot rob satan's kingdom without first binding satan. Only then can his demons be cast out." (Matthew 12:29, Living Bible)

Q. So what is the first thing you are to do when you pray for someone?
A. *Matthew 12:29a* tells you to bind satan.

Q. Why?
A. You bind satan in order that his demons can be cast out.

When you pray, you move in as a Weapon in the Hands of God, taking from satanic dominion that which he once possessed.

A. "Father, in Jesus' name, I bind satan in (whatever, whomever)."
   1. Resist to release, or peace.
   2. Stand then in faith.
   3. Share the testimony of the victory, thereby breaking doubt or fear, (the opposite of faith.)
   It is not you binding satan, but you giving God the entrance to the stronghold, destroying the enemy, *(II Chron. 16:9).*

B. Pray aggressively/offensively.
   1. Don't plead with the enemy.
   2. Attack the enemy in prayer.
   3. There are no scriptures of defense in the New Testament. They are all offensive in position.

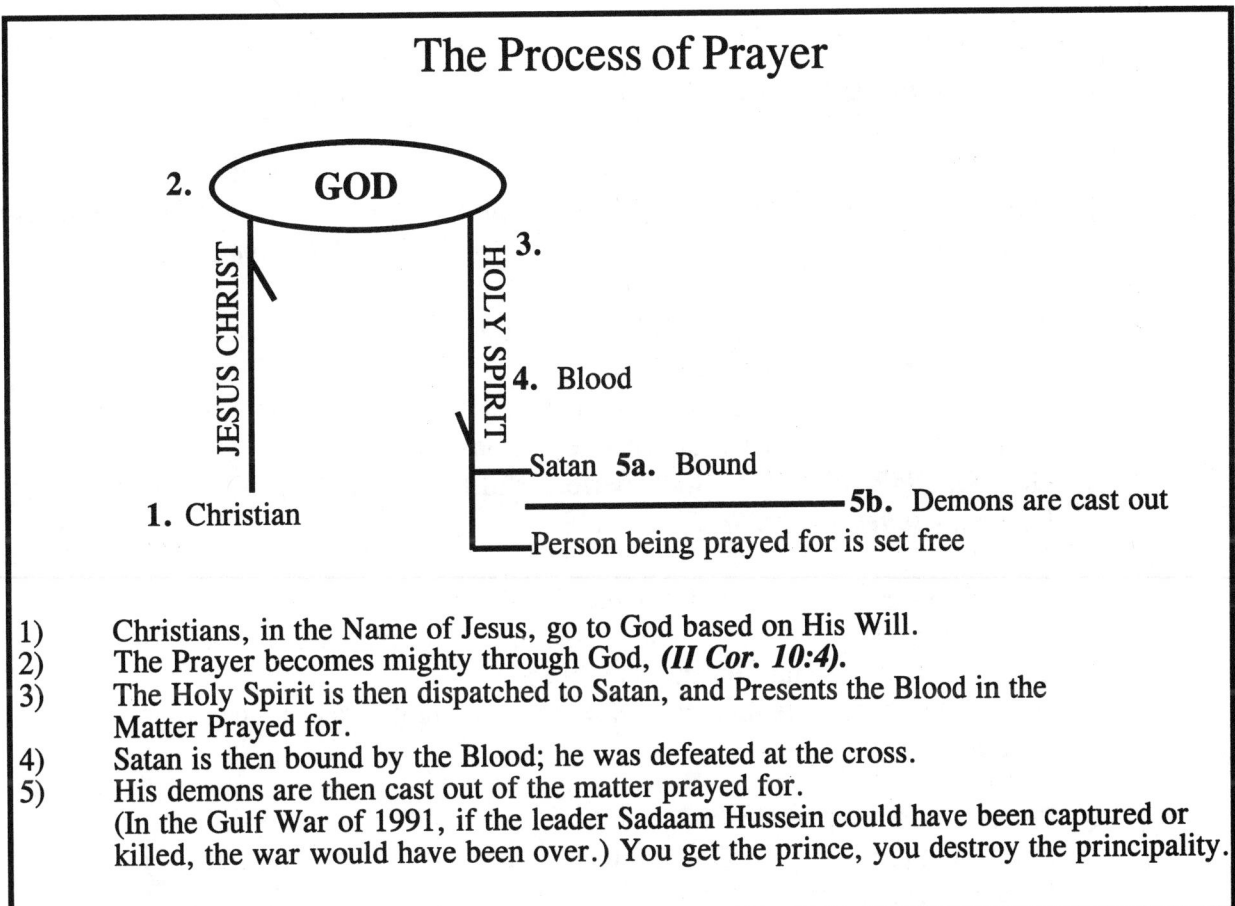

The Process of Prayer

1)   Christians, in the Name of Jesus, go to God based on His Will.
2)   The Prayer becomes mighty through God, *(II Cor. 10:4).*
3)   The Holy Spirit is then dispatched to Satan, and Presents the Blood in the Matter Prayed for.
4)   Satan is then bound by the Blood; he was defeated at the cross.
5)   His demons are then cast out of the matter prayed for.
   (In the Gulf War of 1991, if the leader Sadaam Hussein could have been captured or killed, the war would have been over.) You get the prince, you destroy the principality.

C. Never take spiritual instruction from someone who speaks negatively, or who listens to a negative report, *(Proverbs 6:12, 17:4, I Peter 3:5-8 Amp.).*
   Pr. 6:12 A naughty person, a wicked man, walketh with a froward mouth. The Hebrew word for "naughty" is "beliyaal" = "controlled by satan."

ALWAYS REMEMBER, satan's ministry is to divide. He does this by negative, critical confession. You lose your victory by what comes out of your mouth, *(Matt. 15:11)*. You are instructed to never return evil for evil, but to pray in deliverance for those who speak evil, negative words. Your prayer against satan in their lives is for welfare, happiness, and protection. 1) Welfare in the kingdom of God; for they are destitute. 2) Happiness; for they are without joy. 3) Protection; satan enters into the Christian life through the negative speech of the Christian. It is not what goes into a person's mouth that defiles him, but what comes out, *(I Peter 3:8 - 10 Amp.)*.

SEE BROTHER BONNER'S BOOK GOD'S ANSWER TO THE CRITICAL CHRISTIAN - **KYMS**.

THE SAME MIRACLE THROUGH DIFFERENT EYES

V.   *LUKE 11:20-22*

> *20 But if I with the finger of God cast out devils, no doubt the kingdom of God is come upon you.*
> *21 When a strong man armed keepeth his palace, his goods are in peace:*
> *22 But when a stronger than he shall come upon him, and overcome him, he taketh from him all his armor wherein he trusted, and divideth his spoils.*

A. You are to point *"...the finger of God..."* at a burden, *(Luke 11:20)*.
    1. The *"finger"* of God is the Holy Spirit.
        a. When you pray the will of God you point the Holy Spirit into the matter.
        b. The Holy Spirit binds satan and his demons flee.
    2. The *"Kingdom of God"* is God's perfect Will for your life, as it is written in Heaven, *(Ephesians 2:10)*.

B. God enters a circumstance only through prayer or judgment.
    1. "Father, in Jesus' name, I bind satan in (whatever, whomever)." Then...
    2. Stand in praise until the answer comes.
    3. Again pray for one thing at a time, to the point of "release, peace or report."

Q. What is the Finger of God?
A. The Holy Spirit. Every individual that has been saved is the product of another Christian's prayer.

"If I with the Finger of God cast out devils, no doubt the Kingdom of God has come upon you."

Q. How are you to Pray?
A. Father in the name of Jesus, I bind satan in... (Remember, you are not binding but you are agreeing with God and bringing Him into the matter.)

Q. How does God get into a matter?
A. Prayer.

Q. How many things are you to pray for at a time?
A. One, in Warfare Prayer.

When you pray and get an answer, it is evident that the Kingdom of God is upon you.

C. You cannot pray without God's Power, *(Luke 11:21)*.
1. The strongman is satan. When he is in control of a situation there is nothing but the power of God that can destroy him.
2. Have you ever tried to talk to a son, daughter, neighbor or friend about Jesus and, though deep in sin, he/she would say, "I'm all right, leave me alone. Don't bother me." You cannot reach this person on a head-to-head level. He/she bound.
   a. Don't try to go "head on" with anyone (vis-a-vis salvation).
   b. Pray the matter through first according to *II Cor. 4:3,4,* binding satan to the point of release.
   c. You, in your strength, are no match for the enemy. You must pray, thereby bringing the Holy Spirit into the matter.
   d. Sin was destroyed at the cross by the blood of Jesus Christ, thereby bringing satan's defeat.

Q. Who is the strongman?
A. Satan.

Satan is the god of this world, *(II Cor. 4:4)*. You, therefore, cannot accomplish a thing by your own power or knowledge.

Pray! For it is <u>God</u> that defeats satan.

Q. How does God get into the matter?
A. Prayer.

3. When you pray you bring Christ's Blood into the matter, thereby destroying the power of satan. Through prayer warfare you overcome him.
   But when a stronger power than he comes upon him, and overcome him, He taketh from him all of his armor, (Luke 11:22).
   a. Satan has armor.
   b. The "stronger than he" is God.
   c. God takes satan's armor away by answering the prayer, and divides his spoils. (The victory or peace comes to the individual praying, at the time that the prayer is offered.)

D. Jesus overcomes satan and strips satan of all his armor!!! *(Luke 11:22)*

VI. How Can You Have Answered Prayer?

A. You must be saved, *(John 9:31).*
B. You must be in right standing with God.
C. You must have faith in Jesus Christ, having gone to the Father.
D. You must be armored when you pray. Then you destroy or capture the pieces of armor when you pray. They are the "spoils" of war, *(Luke 11:22).*

You Must Pray in Authority. You are called a...

Warrior - *I Tim. 1:18*
Avenger - through prayer bringing God into the matter - *Rom. 12:19*
Soldier - *II Tim. 2:3*
Overcomer - *I John 4:4, Revelation 12:11*
Intercessor - *Rom. 8:26*
Weapon in the hands of God - *Eph. 6:14-18*
Ambassador - *II Cor 5:20*

Not one of these has a defensive posture in them. They are all OFFENSIVE!!!
Therefore, you as a Christian should attack, for satan is a defeated foe.

If God does not answer your prayers, you are worthless in the kingdom of God, *"saved so as by fire," (I Cor. 3:15).* For the only evident sign of maturity in the life of the Christian is answered prayer. Hearing the voice of God, understanding the voice of God, and agreeing with the will of God destroys the power of satan.

"ALL PRAYER IS WARFARE"

SECTION TWO

I. *"MEN OUGHT ALWAYS TO PRAY AND NOT TO FAINT" (LUKE 18:1 KVJ).*

A. The Greek for "faint," "ekkakeo," means to "fail in heart." The Amplified translates this as, you ***"ought always to pray... and not give up."*** We are not to give up!
   1. God will answer in your spirit (release or peace), *(I John 5:14-15 Amp).*

B. You are to pray aggressively, *(II Corinthians 10:3-5 - James 5:16).*

C. You are to pray constantly.
   1. In Warfare Prayer, Pray for one issue at a time, doing battle one at a time.
   2. Wait for the "release" that the issue is settled. The old-time saints called it "praying through," or "deliverance,"
   (Matt. 6:13 Amp.) *"Deliver us from the evil one."*

   I John 5:14-15 (Amplified)

   14 And this is the confidence - the assurance, [the privilege of] boldness - which we have in Him: [we are sure] that if we ask anything (make any request according to His Will (in agreement with His own plan) He listens to and hears us.
   15 And if (since) we [positively] know that He listens to us in whatever we ask, we also know [with settled and absolute knowledge] that we have [granted us as our present possessions] the requests made of Him.

These two verses are the spring-board to God's answering when you pray. The first position is praying the Mind or Will of God. Once you have established your position from a burden or agreement, *(Matthew 16:18, 18:18-19),* you then can come in boldness. The scripture gives you the statement, the "privilege of boldness," that you have in Him. Once you agree with His own plan, He listens to and hears you.

Then, because you are praying His Will, you exercise your faith. Therefore, you know that you have given to us, as your present possessions, the requests made of Him. It is granted as you pray, and you know it by the peace or release.

Q. How long are you to pray?
A. Until the Answer comes.

The passive Christian is in bondage. The aggressive Christian is free and sets free. Quit going to people for prayer. Go to God, until you get your answer or release! Ask God that whatever it takes to bring you to a place of answered prayer that He would do it.

II. Jesus shocks His listeners by the use of *"Judge," Luke 18:2a.*

Many times Jesus taught by the "adrenaline" method or shock therapy. He would use an analogy to get their attention. Such was the case when teaching prayer to His disciples. He caught their attention by using circumstances in their present day. Just as they hated their tax collectors, (Jews who had sold out to the Romans,) so they hated even more their Judges who wielded greater power and authority. To open their eyes to prayer warfare, He, in this teaching, caused the judge to be completely corrupt in order to stir up their anger. Then He made His point in prayer. How many times in our own lives are we brought to tribulation to develop God's Will in our own lives?

"Saying, There was in a city a judge...," Luke 2:18a

A. Anger very likely prevented the disciples from hearing the word *"Judge."*
1. They (the Judges) were corrupt.
2. They were Jews chosen by Romans.
3. Judges were non religious: reprobates/mercenaries receiving a percentage of the settlement in the cases brought before them.
4. They were traitors to Jews and their traditions, (even though the Judges chosen by the Romans were Jews).

At that time, the Judge was a Jewish man, chosen by the Romans. Therefore, this man was considered a traitor by his people, the Jews. He was seen as a mercenary, someone loyal to the Romans and not the Jews, interested only in wealth and power. The Jewish people hated their Judges.

B. This Judge, as Jesus described him, was especially loathsome.
1. He did not "fear" or believe in God, (No reverential awe). *Luke 18:2b "...which feared not God..."* This meant that not only did this Judge not fear God, but he was committed only to Roman law. He would use nothing in Levitical law, that was traditional among the Jews in regard to his judgments.
2. Christ further added in *Luke 18:2c "...neither regarded man."* This meant that this man was a hanging Judge, whereby sentencing could mean death on the cross for the defendant, for breaking Roman Law.

C. In *verse 3*, Jesus includes a *"widow"* in the scenario.

> *3 And there was a widow in that city; and she came unto him, saying, "Avenge me of mine adversary."*

In that time period the term *"widow"* meant that this woman had no male covering, or heirs. In that particular system, if a woman had no male representatives, which also meant "income," this Judge especially would not be interested. At this point Christ's listeners really became incensed, for they hated their judges.
1. The widow had no one to represent her.
2. Because she had nothing, and because she was a woman, the Judge did not want to hear her case.
3. But, the widow was constantly petitioning the Judge to avenge her. (The Greek word for "avenge" is "ekaideo" meaning "revenge").

   Then Jesus added in the last part of *verse 3* that the widow kept stating *"...Avenge me of mine adversary."*

D. The Greek word for *"adversary"* in *Luke 18:3 (KJV)* is "antidikos" - satan. When the listeners heard Him use the word antidikos, (satan), they suddenly realized He was telling them how to deal with the adversary, (satan), through Prayer, (Warfare).

E. In your life, God cannot enter into your situation except through prayer. God wants someone through whom He can show Himself strong.
(II Chronicles 16:9) "For the eyes of the LORD run to and fro throughout the whole earth, to shew himself strong in the behalf of [them] whose heart [is] perfect toward him...."

Again, this can only happen by prayer.

F. Here is Christ's scenario of the Judge and the Widow.
   1. It could be described/shown in this way:

   Judge (no fear of God - no regard for man)

   Widow   **Adversary** who had created an offense.

The only person that had the power to help the widow was the Judge. He desired to do nothing about her situation because there was no monetary gain for his effort. If he were to rule, his decision would bring relief to the widow who was being wronged. Jesus used this analogy to first stir up the hearing of His disciples. He then used this analogy to explain the purpose and power of prayer.

Using the same type of analogy as Christ did, we will use you the reader as the beginning of this illustration. The scenario could be that satan has your son/daughter in bondage. In that case you go to God in prayer.

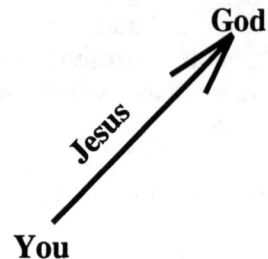

Go to God in the <u>name of Jesus</u>. He is your Advocate or defense attorney. As in the case of the Widow and the Judge who had authority over her adversary, so does God in prayer have authority over satan, your adversary. Again, Prayer works, based on God's Will when you go to God in the name of Jesus Christ. The Holy Spirit is then dispatched into the presence of satan who is not omnipresent, (all places at all times). He presents the Blood of Jesus in the matter for which you are praying. Satan is bound. The demons assigned to the person or situation are then cast out, *(Matt. 12:27-28)*.

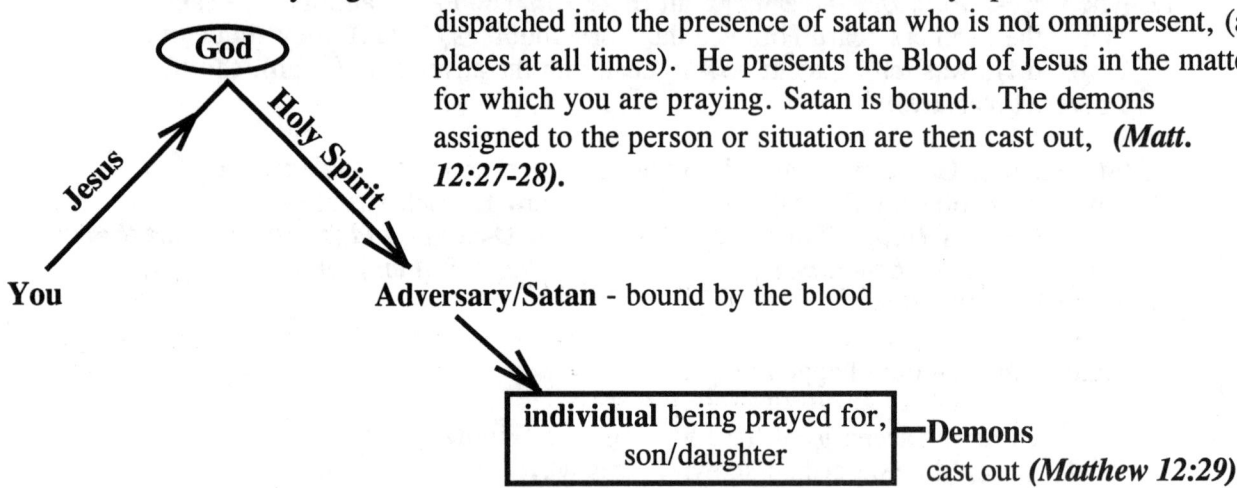

Again it could be prayed - "Father in the Name of Jesus Christ, I bind satan in (<u>Give Name</u>). Remember, it is not you binding satan. It is by prayer warfare that God through prayer destroys the works of the devil, *(I John 3:8)*.

Consider the process of having to go to court. A judge and attorney must be chosen in order for your case to continue. But in the spirit realm Jesus is your attorney. His availability to you is immediate. Upon your "court date," you find your accuser and adversary, satan, ready. He has captured your son or daughter in deep bondage. He is ready to prosecute based on his evidence against him/her. Instead of waiting your turn on the docket, Jesus goes directly to the Judge and insists that you come boldly with Him. When He reaches the Judge, (God), He says, "I want to introduce you to one of your children." God says, "I recognize this child, he/she is covered in the Blood." *(Hebrews 10:19)*

Satan then looks up and sees you in the presence of the Judge. He knows at that moment that his case against the person he has bound is over. He is bound and his demons must flee. Your prayer burden is relieved and delivered.

That is how prayer warfare works.

Luke 18:4-7

> 4 *And he would not for a while: but afterward he said within himself, Though I fear not God, nor regard man;*
> 5 *Yet because this widow troubleth me, I will avenge her, lest by her continual coming she weary me.*
> 6 *And the Lord said, Hear what the unjust judge saith.*
> 7 *And shall not God avenge his own elect, which cry day and night unto him, though he bear long with them?*

III. HOW LONG DOES IT TAKE FOR THE FATHER TO JUDGE AGAINST THE ADVERSARY? (LUKE 18:8)

> 8 *I tell you that he will avenge them speedily. Nevertheless when the Son of man cometh, shall he find faith on the earth?*

A. God avenges *"speedily."* The Greek word "Tachos" means "shortly or quickly" *(v.8).*
   1. You don't have to pound at Him day and night. (Prevailing Prayer disposes of the doctrine of "wearing God down" to answer prayers.)
   2. If He doesn't answer, ask the question, "Father in the name of Jesus Christ, what is wrong in my life that keeps me from hearing from you?"

The inner working of the Holy Spirit directs the Christian in what to pray, *(Romans 8:26-27).* In *Luke 18:7,8* you face the doctrine of prevailing prayer. Christ's statement in the seventh verse seems to say that if the elect (Christian) persists in an issue He will finally give in. However, you find in the end of *verse 7* a question mark. Therefore, He is answering His own question by declaring in *verse 8* that He will answer *speedily.*

B. How much power is involved when you pray?
   1. All that God is according to your faith.
   2. It involves everything you believe about the name of Jesus and what He will do when you pray. (*Hebrews 11:1* Faith is the evidence that produces substance.)

   Q. How long does it take the Father to judge against the Adversary?

   A. _____.

Q. How much power is involved when you Pray?

A. _____ .

C. Again, what is faith?
    1. What you believe the name of Jesus Christ will do having gone to the Father when you use it.
    2. Faith is thanking Jesus in advance for what He is yet going to do based on His Will. (It is the report of *Hebrews 11*).

IV.   WHAT PART DOES PRAISE HAVE IN ANSWERED PRAYER?

A. When you pray, you attack the same with Praise, *(Psalm 149:6)*.
    1. Always be offensive. Prayer is Warfare!
    2. There is no defensive perimeter in the New Testament, even the armor of *Ephesians 6* protects the warrior who is facing the enemy and is on the offensive. You are commanded to hunger, thirst, seek, knock, strain, pursue, chase, assault with violence *(Matthew 11:12)*, labor to enter into rest. Every verse has you going after Christ. You are to be aggressive in warfare.

The passive Christian is in bondage. The aggressive Christian is free and sets free.

B. When you were saved you received all of the Holy Spirit. When you are filled He gets all of you, *(I Corinthians 12:13 - Ephesians 5:18)*.
    1. How much of you does He have?
    2. You are continually to be filled with the Spirit of God, *(Ephesians 5:18)*.

18 And be not drunk with wine, wherein is excess; but be ye being filled with the Spirit; (Amp.)

To be filled with the Spirit means to have come to a place in your life where you have completely given over to God's will in your life. Then, He who dwells within comes to cover you without. You then are led of the Spirit. You walk in the Spirit. It is at this level that God's Will begins to be performed through your life.

Prayer is not the position of the body, but is God's Will working through you as written in heaven, *(Ephesians 2:10)*.

C. What happens when you become filled with (empowered by) the Holy Spirit?
    1. The Spirit takes control.
    2. Your flesh is under control, *(Romans 12:1-2)*.
    3. The soul submits to the Spirit. The body therefore becomes the vehicle of ministry.
    4. The physical becomes a servant of the Spirit, (according to the Will of the Spirit).

D. The Holy Spirit always points you to Jesus.
   1. The Spirit never glorifies Himself.
   2. Jesus always sought to bring glory to God the Father by extending God's Will
       and Ministry to earth through His prayers.

   Q. What are you to do when you Pray?
   A. Attack! There is no defensive posture in the New Testament.

V. **PRAISE IS THE CATALYST TO PRAYER VICTORY. HIGH PRAISE = A TWO - EDGED SWORD.**

   A. Praise is an essential part of prayer. It is declaring the victory before you enter into the
       battle, *(Psalm 149 KJV)*.

Psalm 149

1 *Praise ye the LORD. Sing unto the LORD a new song, [and] his praise in the
   congregation of saints.*
2 *Let Israel rejoice in him that made him: let the children of Zion be joyful in their King.*
3 *Let them praise his name in the dance: let them sing praises unto him with the
   timbrel and harp.*
4 *For the LORD taketh pleasure in his people: he will beautify the meek with salvation.*
5 *Let the saints be joyful in glory: let them sing aloud upon their beds.*
6 *[Let] the high [praises] of God [be] in their mouth, and a two-edged sword in their hands;*
7 *To execute vengeance upon the heathen, [and] punishments upon the people;*
8 *To bind their kings with chains, and their nobles with fetters of iron;*
9 *To execute upon them the judgment written: this honour have all his saints. Praise ye
   the LORD.*

   B. Praise occurs when you reach for God, *(Psalm 149:6)*.

   C. High praise is when God reaches down and inhabits your praises and ministers through
       you. *For we [Christians] are the true circumcision, who worship God in spirit and by
       the Spirit of God, and exult and glory and pride ourselves in Jesus Christ, and
       put no confidence or dependence [on what we are] in the flesh and on outward
       privileges and physical advantages and external appearances, (Philippians 3:3 Amp.).*

       The Bible says you worship Him *"in the Spirit and by the Spirit."* Have you ever felt
       oppression? Oppression is satan moving on you. You begin to give in to your
       circumstances rather than attacking the situation with praise, leading to high praise.
       You then open your mouth and declare how negative the situation is. At that moment
       you become depressed. Satan's pressure causes you to see only your circumstance.
       Oppression is when he is moving on you. Depression is when he is sitting on you.
       You can break out! God gives you *"the garment of praise for the Spirit of heaviness,"*
       (Isa. 61:3).

Q. What do you do when you pray?

A. Praise.

Q. What do you do when you praise?

A. Attack. You become aggressive. "How dare satan touch me or my loved ones." You continue to praise until you sense release or peace.

VI. NOW, YOU MUST UNDERSTAND THAT SATAN ENTERS YOUR LIFE THROUGH YOUR CONFESSION.

A. Stop confessing negatives about yourself or others and start thanking God for what He's doing.

B. Satan and his demons hear your Negitive Confession and set up *"wiles"* to drag you down, *(Ephesians 6:10 - 11, James 3:6).*

And the tongue [is] a fire, a world of iniquity: so is the tongue among our members, that it defileth the whole body, and setteth on fire the course of nature; and it is set on fire of hell, (James 3:6).

Also see *Matthew 15:11*

C. **Do not dwell on bad circumstances.**
   1. *In everything give thanks, James 1:2-5 (Amp.).*
   2. *Consider it wholly joyful, my brethren, whenever you are enveloped in or encounter trials of any sort, or fall into various temptation.*
   3. *Be assured and understand that the trial and proving of your faith bring out endurance and steadfastness and patience.*
   4. *But let endurance and steadfastness and patience have full play and do thorough work, so that you may be [people] perfectly and fully developed with no defects, lacking in nothing.*

D. **Don't gossip or listen to it.** In *Proverbs 6:12 and 17:4,* "naughty" means "belial" or "satan".

E. **Praise God in everything.** (Again, satan enters into your life through your confession.)

Don't look at your circumstances and beg God to get involved. Look to God and He will involve Himself in your circumstances.

VII. WHO BRINGS *"VENGEANCE UPON THE HEATHEN"*? PSALM 149:7

7 To execute vengeance upon the heathen, [and punishments upon the people]

A. Vengeance is brought upon the demonic strongholds by warfare, faith praying. *"Vengeance is mine thus sayeth the Lord,"* (Romans 12:19). God gets into the matter by prayer as you discovered with the widow.

B. Answered prayer should be an every day experience.

C. In *Psalm 149:7*, *"heathen"* and *"people"* refer to spirit beings, not humans.

D. When you pray, you bind satan. When you bind satan his demons are cast out of the situation. *"To bind their kings with chains, and their nobles with fetters of iron..."* *Psalm 149:8.*

In this verse, the Hebrew word for "kings" is "melek," which means "gods." (Satan is the god of this world). *Ephesians 6:12* states that *"we wrestle not against flesh and blood but against principalities."* You bind the prince when you move into high praise.

E. When you pray (aggressively), you bind the king. His kingdom is then defeated.

    Q. What are You to do when you pray?
    A. Bind their kings with chains, (high praise does this), and their nobles with fetters of iron. This is what happens when you pray in faith, believing.

VIII. SATAN IS ALREADY DEFEATED (JUDGED BY GOD).

A. We execute judgment, (or "carry out the death sentence") by praise or faith affirmation, *Psalm 149:8.*

    9 To execute upon them the judgment written: this honour have all his saints. Praise ye the LORD.

In this case, satan has already received judgment at the cross. His power was defeated by the Blood of Jesus Christ. It is as one who has been judged, given the death penalty and is now sitting in the electric chair. When you pray in faith, which is the will of God to bind satan, you "pull the switch." Satan's judgment is already written.

B. Prayer is what Jesus used to destroy the works of darkness.
    1. He prayed the mind of the Father.
    2. The Father became operational through the Son, *(I John 3:8).*

C. Pray, "Father in the name of Jesus, I bind satan in (whatever) / (whomever)," and then begin to praise Him that it's done until you sense the peace or release.

God says satan is already defeated by the finished work of the Cross.

    Q. How does God get into a matter?
    A. Prayer.

When God gets into the matter satan runs scared, as the defeated foe that he is. God's people must pray in order that God can get into a matter and execute judgment on satan.

Then the verse declares...

"This honor hath all His saints."

If you are a Christian, you have the honor of having answered prayer. There is no greater honor.

Q. Is your Spouse in Bondage?
Q. Is your family in Bondage?   WHY???
Q. Are you in Bondage?

ANSWERED PRAYER BRINGS HONOR TO GOD.

PRAISE YE THE LORD. [FAITH AFFIRMATION.]

"CONDUCTING WARFARE PRAYER"

SECTION THREE

I. INTRODUCTION: THE DOOR TO CONDUCTING WARFARE PRAYER

Our third step in Warfare Praying is to bring you to a place to hear from God in the inner man.

We are showing you that Christ is alive and does speak to the inner man through the Holy Spirit.

He does this by the Holy Spirit that lives in your spirit. God will conduct His will through your life. He will open the Truth of Himself to you. This is the reason why I say that when you pray you are to pray until the report or release of *Hebrews 11* becomes manifest, or until peace comes with the Truth of God's inspiration in your spirit.

"Call unto me and I will answer thee," Jeremiah 33:3; "...roll your works unto the Lord, commit and trust them wholly unto Him, and He will cause your thoughts to become agreeable to His Will and so shall your plans be established and succeed," Proverb 16:3 (Amp).

So the true process of prayer is your mind coming into agreement with the Spirit of God, *Philippians 2:5, Romans 12:1, 2* that your mind becomes His mind. True prayer is God's Will through your life at the level of your faith.

Please understand, for those of you who want to mature in God, every verse of scripture in the New Testament that deals with your relationship with Christ instructs you to pursue Him. You are to hunger, seek, strain, pursue, thirst, chase, violently assault. You are not to wait for Christ to move into your life. You are to go after Him. You are to "labor to enter into rest..."

"For we are God's [own] handiwork (His workmanship), recreated in Christ Jesus, [born anew] that we may do those good works which God predestined (planned beforehand) for us, (taking paths which He prepared ahead of time) that we should walk in them, living the good life which He prearranged and made ready for us to live," Ephesians 2:10 (Amp).

This verse of scripture tells you that you are to take the path by which He ministers and manifests Himself through your life. By that activity the Will of God is completed according to His purpose for you. Every Christian in God's Will is living out the day that Christ has written out before Heaven even began. He wrote out the order for your life and that which He would do through you, based on foreknowledge, having seen that you would be saved. He then planned out the activity of Christ through you. You see, true Christianity is the activity of Christ through you. Religion is the activity of Christians doing Christian activity. So leaders teach carnal Christians certain principles, or how to live within a framework of denominational principles. If they live these out they are, by their denominational standards, good Christians. But that is not so. Beloved, you are to be filled with Christ. You are to operate in His Will. He, through you, will bring the dynamics of His life to break the hindrances of satan. That is all your life is. Prayer is not the position of the body, but the condition of the Heart. Prayer is the activity of God through man. That is why He instructs you to, *"pray without ceasing."* That does not mean that you are to be on your knees 24 hours a day. It means to be so coupled with Christ, pressing towards Him with your life, going after Him with all your heart that when you break through from flesh to Spirit, you are no longer conformed to this world, *(Romans 12:2)*. Now the word *"conformed"* does not mean "not to dance," "not to drink," "not to do this or that," but that God's laws will be kept by His Grace in your spirit. It means *"to be transformed."* Back in that day in time they were circumcising their male children to prove that they were Christians. Conformity is not the circumcision of the flesh. It is the cutting away of the "old man," by the circumcision of the heart. This occurs when you begin to actively pursue Jesus, going after Him with all of your might. He cuts those things away from you and the life of Christ manifests Himself through you. The Bible says *"...be ye not conformed to this world but be ye transformed by the renewing of your mind..."* Therefore, you come to transformation by the mind of Christ, which is from the point of the activity of your faith. If you studied the first of this series you saw that you move from praise to high praise. Praise is when you reach for God. High praise is when He is reaching through you. Praise, Beloved, is when you are conformed, literally. High praise is when you are transformed. At that point His mind becomes your mind, that you can agree. It is at that point that the Spirit of God moves. That is DEEP, but we are going to be dealing with the issue on the basis of praying in Warfare... by the Spirit.

II. YOU MUST HEAR FROM GOD IN THE INNER MAN.

A. Christ is alive and does speak to the inner man, *(Ephesians 1:17,18)*.

1. In your spirit, God will conduct His Will through your life, *(Matthew 6:9,10)*.
2. God normally does not speak in an audible voice, *(Romans 8:26,27)*.

B. He will open the truth of Himself to you.

1. Pray to the report, until your faith has become substance, *(Hebrews 11:1)*.
2. Pray until peace comes, *(Luke 18:1)*.
3. *Hebrews 5:14, Proverb 16:3, Jeremiah 33:3 (Amplified)*

C. The process of prayer is allowing the Spirit of God to become your mind.
(Philippians 2:5, Romans 12:1,2)
1. All the days of your life have already been planned out from the day you were born again, *(Ephesians 2:10 Amplified)*.
2. You must find the mind of God through answered prayer in order to bring that plan into completion.
3. Religion is man adhering with varying degrees of success to a set of principles. There are over 20,000 denominations worldwide.
4. Christianity is Jesus living His life through a yielded believer, *(Colossians 1:27)*.

D. Again, prayer is not the position of the body but the condition of the heart.
   1. You are to be filled with Christ, *(Ephesians 5:18).*
   2. Prayer is the activity of God through man, as the Holy Spirit conforms him from the inside out to the person of Christ.
      a. You are to pray without ceasing, practicing the presence of Christ constantly.
      b. The believer is to be so "in tune" with Jesus that he can hear his voice intuitively. Then, "When in doubt, don't!"
   3. As you constantly pursue Jesus, the "old man" is replaced with Jesus' life through you in a growing position.
      (Hebrews 12:14, " follow" in the Greek is, "dioko," meaning "to pursue" or "chase" Jesus Christ.)
   4. From there, weights, or sins that beset you, are laid aside.

   You Are Not To Be Conformed To This World But Transformed By The Renewing Of Your Mind, (Romans 12:2).

E. Praise is God's method of re-establishing the Holy Spirit's control when you reach for God, *(Psalm 149:6).*

F. High praise is God reaching through you.
   1. God's mind becomes your mind.
   2. At that point, you can agree with His mind.
   3. Then the Spirit of God moves, *(Philippians 3:3 Amplified).*

G. All prayer is warfare!

III. BACKGROUND TO *MATTHEW 16:13-19*

Jesus was in a Place called Banyez, or "the Cave of Pan," next to the city of Ceasera Phillipi, teaching His Disciples about Prayer.

This location is at the base of Mount Herman. There are three springs that feed into the Jordan River. This is one of those outlets. There is a cave located there called the Cave of Pan, where those who followed after the god Pan came to worship. It is cool inside with an abundance of fig trees and cold water from the spring. This very likely is the cave where Jesus met with His disciples at that time.

When Jesus came into the coasts of Caesarea Philippi, He asked His disciples, saying, *"...Whom do men say that I the Son of man am?" MATTHEW 16:13*

The Disciples responded by giving Christ a myriad of dead prophets that the public was claiming was Christ...

14 And they said, Some [say that thou art] John the Baptist: some, Elias, and other, Jeremias, or one of the prophets.

Jesus replied in *Matthew 16:15-18*

15 He saith unto them, But whom say ye that I am?

Jesus wanted to know what their own personal thoughts were, not what the public was thinking…

16 And Simon Peter answered and said, Thou art the Christ, the Son of the living God.

This was a declaration / proclamation. This was not hearsay. It was not in evidence of what he had seen, but it was the Holy Spirit of God speaking through Peter, and Jesus heard the speaking of the Father…

17 And Jesus answered and said unto him, Blessed art thou, Simon Barjona: for flesh and blood hath not revealed [it] unto thee, but my Father which is in heaven.

Jesus was telling Peter that he had a wonderful experience. To this point it had to be the Greatest Experience in His Life. For he was able to hear from the Father by the Holy Spirit and proclaim what he had heard.

What actually happened to Peter happens to all Christians when they pray the Will of God. The Holy Spirit spoke through his mouth declaring Christ the Messiah. True prayer is the mind of God through the mouth or heart of man. Also, the Holy Spirit had not yet come and would not inhabit the Christian until *Acts 2:1-4.* So the experience of Peter was even more startling to Jesus as He heard the voice of His Father through Peter. The Holy Spirit has been sent to the earth for one reason and that is to declare Jesus as the Messiah. Thus, answered prayer is the continued ministry of Christ through you by the Holy Spirit.

Then Jesus declared…   *18 And I say also unto thee, That thou art Peter, and upon this rock I will build my church; and the gates of hell shall not prevail against it.*

verse 18, tells you that the gates of hell shall not prevail against you - not you, but God in you. The Christian is the Church, His body, His bride.

verse 18 - The gates of hell shall not prevail against (the Church).

Then, Jesus states, *"Thou art Peter and upon this Rock I will build my Church."*

Jesus said: *Peter -* this means "Petros" or "small Piece of Stone" - *and upon this Rock -* which means "Petra" or "mountain of stone" - *I will build my CHURCH!*

You can declare yourself a piece of stone on the basis of the fact that you are a born again child of God. A piece of the Rock. You are a "chip off the ol' block!!!"

THE GATES OF HELL CANNOT PREVAIL AGAINST A PRAYING BELIEVER, OR CHURCH
(Matthew 16:18)

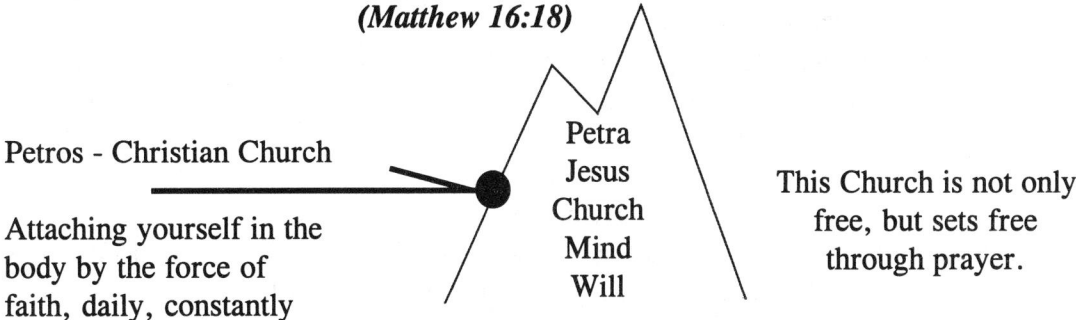

Petros - Christian Church

Attaching yourself in the
body by the force of
faith, daily, constantly

Petra
Jesus
Church
Mind
Will

This Church is not only
free, but sets free
through prayer.

A. It is not you that the gates of hell are not prevailing against. It is Jesus, when you are in Him...
    1. You (of yourself) have no authority.
    2. Your authority is "in Jesus" at the level of your faith.

B. Prayer brings God into the matter.

C. The *"keys"* as you will see, are literally the "mind of Christ," *(v.19).*

19 And I will give unto thee the keys of the kingdom of heaven: and whatsoever thou shalt bind on earth shall be bound in heaven: and whatsoever thou shalt loose on earth shall be loosed in heaven.

Christ said at this point that He would give Peter the keys to the kingdom.

Keys to the Kingdom = the Mind of Christ

In order for you to understand the Will of God, to be able to agree with it to destroy the works of the devil, you must first have the mind of Christ. His mind becomes active in you when you pursue Christ with all of your heart...

The key to praying is being able to Hear. You must be able to hear and agree in order for God to answer prayer.

> >REMEMBER, GOD ANSWERS NO PRAYERS BUT HIS OWN! < < *verse 19 ...what is already bound and loosed in heaven.* And in *James 5:16,* the word "effectual" = "God praying to God"

YOU CANNOT CHANGE GOD'S MIND!!!

D. You cannot change God's Will or God's mind.
    1. You must agree with God's mind.
    2. This brings God's light into a circumstance and dispels the demonic darkness.
    3. The work of the Holy Spirit is to teach you what to pray as you learn His voice within.

E. You can pursue the mind of Christ through prayer for all circumstances.
1. Salvation
2. Deliverance
3. Healing (all kinds - body, soul, spirit, mind, emotion, and will)
4. Fullness (spirit-filled, spirit-controlled life)
    a. Again, faith is what you believe the name of Jesus Christ will do, having gone to the Father when you use it.
    b. Most Christians are babies and can only receive the milk of the word, *(I Corinthians 3:1-5)*. They remain this way all of their Christian lives.

WHEN YOU PRAY YOU ARE TO BRING GOD INTO THE MATTER ACCORDING TO HIS WILL.

Q. Who can destroy the works of the devil?
A. God!

Q. How do you get God into the Matter?
A. Prayer!

Q. How do you overcome the enemy?
A. Prayer!

Q. What does satan fight the most in your Christian life?
A. Prayer!

Remember, there is a price in praying, and that is hearing.

As you go on with God, He establishes you in His kingdom by brokenness. As you pray, you become more familiar with God's Will for your life. Through this, aggressive warfare is established in that you can destroy satan's work by His power, through faith, in prayer.

You Must Pray in Authority, in Faith Believing, Destroying the Works of the Devil. But You must Be Able to Hear, to Receive His Mind.!!!

"Believe that you have it."

Jesus' mind holds the keys to the kingdom, or the will of God. For instance, when you pray for a lost person you cannot save the individual, but you can bring light (God) into his life, *(II Cor 4:3-4)*.

The reason a person is lost is that "satan hath blinded the minds that he cannot see the light of the gospel." As you stand against the darkness, he can be brought to the light to choose. He still must confess his sins, after drawn by conviction, in order to be born again. You are commanded to pray for the lost, *(I Tim. 2:1-4)*.

Matt. 18:18,19 If you are walking with God you can pray for any matter for which there is a burden. God is not the author of confusion. Therefore, your burden is His Will.

If you cannot hear from God, then study the section on "The 5 U's of Unanswered Prayer."

HERE IS WHAT YOU ARE COMMANDED TO DO...

Every morning when you awaken you must again choose whom you will serve. To begin with you are separated from God. This does not mean lost. But by your own choosing you are to bring yourself back to God's Will. Thus is the reason for prayer.

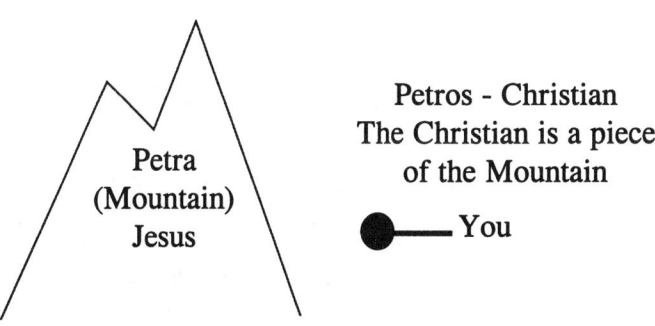

You must daily choose to place your life back into the mountain to work out your salvation, *(Phil. 2:12).*
(God's prewritten plan for your life)

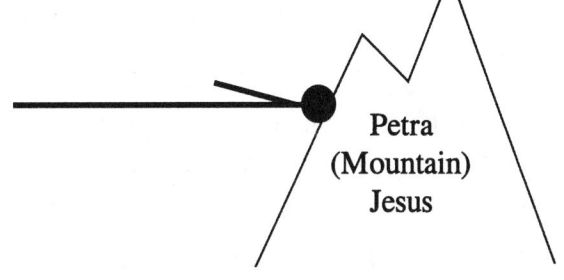

You must fight to gain that position: Hunger, thirst, seek, knock, strain, pursue, assault with violence, labor to enter into that rest, to cease from your own works as God did from His.

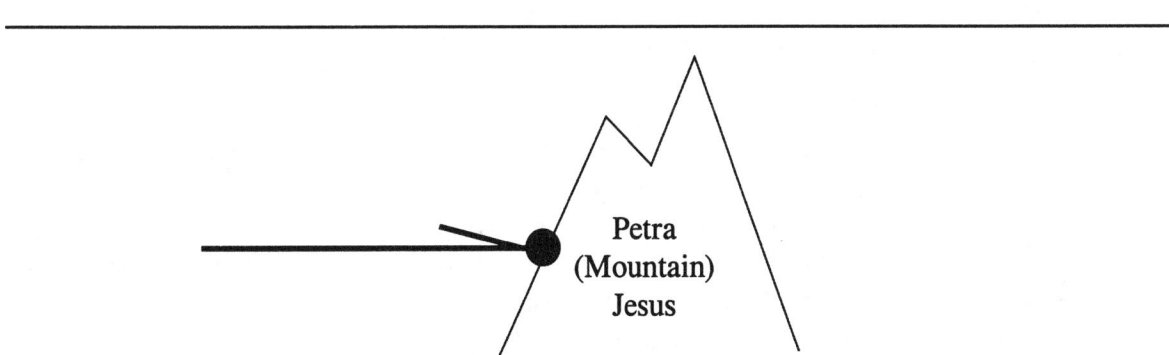

Once positioned back into the mountain you then have the MIND of Christ because you have labored into the position. Another way to say it is that you have given over to the Holy Spirit that which was revealed to you by God's will in Prayer, *(Romans 8:26-27).*

v. 19...And I will give unto Thee the keys to the Kingdom...

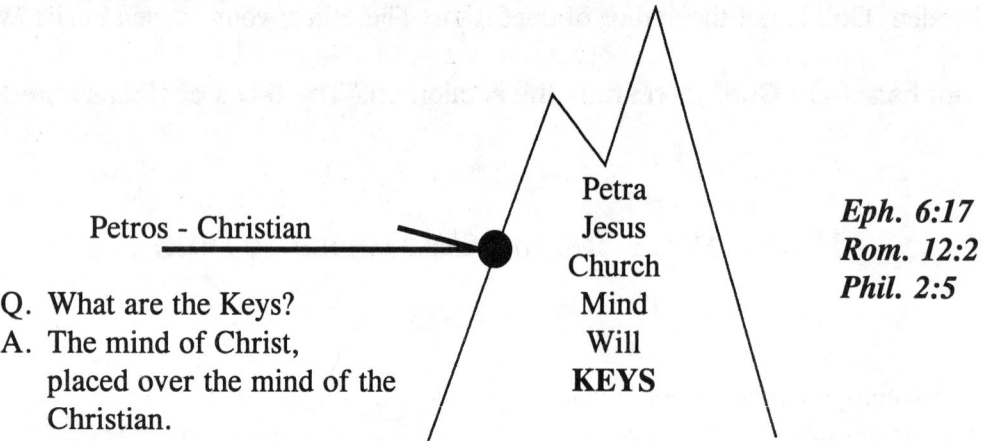

Petros - Christian

Q. What are the Keys?
A. The mind of Christ, placed over the mind of the Christian.

Petra
Jesus
Church
Mind
Will
KEYS

Eph. 6:17
Rom. 12:2
Phil. 2:5

Q. What is the Kingdom of God?

A. It is God's Will for your life as written in Heaven. Therefore when you, as a Christian, fight to regain your walk in Christ and maintain it, the Holy Spirit is free to conduct God's business through you. From this position you then know what to pray for, based on what is bound and loosed. The keys to the kingdom is God's will through you at the level of your faith. The more you drive yourself to Him the more He can accomplish through you, according to His Will. Thus is the work of the Holy Spirit through you. Jesus did not hear the voice of Peter declare Him the Son of God, but he heard the Holy Spirit. Again, He said to Peter the greatest thing that could be said to a Christian. To be in such a position with God that through you the Holy Spirit can declare that Jesus is the Christ, is the power of brokenness praying... *"On earth as it is in heaven."*

IV. CHRIST WILL BUILD HIS TRUE CHURCH IN THIS WAY:

A. "Piece of stone," (petros or small piece), born again believers.
   1. *"upon this rock..."* (Jesus Christ [Petra, Mountain]) *"...I will build My Church."*
   2. The Christian is as Peter: "Petros," a "piece of stone."
   3. Again, at salvation you become a piece of that Rock, (a "chip off the ol' block").

B. Jesus is the Mountain: Petra
   1. You, as a believer are the piece of stone which makes up the mountain, or body of Christ, the Church, *(Eph. 4:11-16).*
   2. Unfortunately, most of the church is so carnal that it cannot hear God's voice by the Holy Spirit that lives within. It separates itself from God's Will, or voice, by not coming to the mountain on a constant basis.
   3. Daily you are to bring your heart back to the mountain: Jesus.
   4. Many verses of scripture instruct you to bring yourself to Him daily. You are to *hunger, thirst, seek, knock, strain, pursue, chase, labor, present yourself,* or better said, Pray.
   5. You must assault with violence the kingdom of God, *(Matthew 11:12* - Greek word "biazo" - the "violent taking by force").
   6. You are to keep yourself in the Will of God so you can hear.
      (You can be saved and still miss God's perfect Will for your life.)

C. God is constantly speaking to the Christian. However...
   1. His children are too fleshly to hear His voice. They must constantly feed on milk, which to the fundamentalists is salvation by grace; to the Charismatics - gifts, *(Hebrews 6:1-3)*.
   2. There must be a return to Him through brokenness to be able to hear once again.
   3. You, the church, must *"pursue"* Jesus at all costs. It is your only hope and the only hope for those who are lost. They will only see Jesus Christ through the warfare praying of others, *(Hebrews 12:14)*.

V.   THE POWER OF TWO IN AGREEMENT, *(MATT. 18:18-19)*.

> *18 Verily I say unto you, Whatsoever ye shall bind on earth shall be bound in heaven: and whatsoever ye shall loose on earth shall be loosed in heaven.*
> *19 Again I say unto you, That if two of you shall agree on earth as touching any thing that they shall ask, it shall be done for them of my Father which is in heaven.*

This begins again with the declaration found in *Matt. 16:19* that you have a right to bind and loose what is already bound and loosed in Heaven. This is only accomplished as you are led of the Holy Spirit, praying the Will of God by burden. Remember, if you are walking with God, a burden is an answered prayer waiting for the catalyst of faith to bring in God's will. In *18:19*, He gives you the Power of agreement with His Will.

"When two agree on earth as touching anything."
1. Remember the *"anything"* follows the sequence of *verse 18.* (His Will) It shall be done for them.
2. Two people in agreement with God's Will are one of the strongest forces in the world. Agreement is the vehicle of God's Will into a matter.
3. This is the principle of the Prayer Assault Teams as you will see in **section 7**. It works. He Works!

VI. TO UNDERSTAND THAT PRAYER IS CHRIST'S MINISTRY THROUGH YOU, YOU MUST SEE THAT JESUS IS THE VINE. YOU ARE THE BRANCH...*(JOHN 15)*.

Christ is the vine. You are the branch. God is the Husbandman. *"...every branch in Me that beareth not fruit He takes away..."* The fruit of a Christian is Christ producing Himself.

If you want to go on with God, and walk in what you hear, the Bible teaches that what you can expect is trouble, a shaking until there is nothing left but Jesus, *(Hebrews 12:27)*.

One of the most important events in the life of the Christian is Tribulation. Tribulation worketh patience, and patience is that revelation of the spirit of God through man. And you can tell at what level you walk with God based on your patience through any matter, *(James 1:2-4 Amp. Ephesians 5:18-20)*.

He is going to purge you, but in the midst of that there will be Glory.

The fruit of a Christian is not soul winning. It is Christ producing Himself through your Prayer, producing souls.
If you have come to the place that the vine - life has become so active, authoritative, dominant, and aggressive, and you are now bringing glory to God in answered prayer, then you are bringing God's glory into man which brings glory to God. In cycle, God looks at you and says, I can trust him with more. You become an even greater, bolder soldier with a greater battlefield, *(Eph. 6:18)*. Prayer Is Warfare!!!

Remember, God answers no prayers but His own. You must have the mind of Christ in order to pray.

If you are operating in principles and not in His Person (Jesus), you are into DEAD works, *(Heb. 6:1).*

I'm not telling you to bail out of your denomination, I'm telling you to run towards Jesus! Then go back to your church and begin to pray in warfare. Bloom where you are planted.

If you abide in Christ and He abides in you, He brings forth much fruit through you.

Q. What is the Fruit of the Christian?
A. It is Jesus Christ Himself.

v.6 If a man abideth not in me, he is cast forth as a branch, and is withered; and men gather them, and cast them into the fire, and they are burned.

That means that your works will be tried. When you gather your life towards men, (religion), your fruit will be dead works. Otherwise, you are not operating by the Spirit.

But if you operate with God, *(John 15:6),* then your works are going to be tried, (As By Fire), *(I Cor 3:15).*

All "precious stones" which will endure are refined by fire.
1. Gold is a product of heat, pressure, minerals.
2. Silver is a product of heat, pressure, and minerals.
3. Diamonds are the strongest of the heat and pressure minerals.
4. God's true work through you, will be after tribulation and refining.

What burns? Wood, hay, stubble: The results of Christians in Christian activity.

What does not burn? Gold, silver, and precious stones: All of these are a product of fire, heat, and pressure.

When you get to the real place of intercession, you meet with "diamond faith." This faith, however, comes only after pruning, *(John 15:2).*

When your works are burned before Christ, He will sift through the ashes and find what is left: gold, silver, precious stones, *(II Cor. 5:10).*

Men who serve in Carnal Christianity will have no works honorable before God. (Nothing Christ did through them.)

Then He Declares...

v.7 if ye abide in me... and My words abide in you...
(the mind of Christ - the Will of God - the Keys to the Kingdom...)

Q. In order to have answered prayer you must be able to do what?
A. Hear.

abide in Me... = attaching yourself to Jesus. Go to God in Prayer. Be filled with the Spirit.

and My words abide in you... = Words of Christ.

ye shall ask... = and it shall be done unto you = Therefore, answered prayer is the mind of Christ being fed through the mind of man. He confesses it through faith and God moves in and does the work.

Q. Is it you asking (ask what you will)?
A. No, it is God asking God through you.

In the Old Testament you are given the promise of the Power of two people in agreement.

Deuteronomy 32:30, Psalm 91:7

One person praying can rout one - thousand demons.
Two persons praying can rout ten - thousand demons.

If they Pray from the Rock (the Ebenezer): the Old Testament Jesus Christ.

Again, *Matthew 18:19*: One person praying, the other person <u>praising</u> in agreement, (this is, *the sword* of *Psalm 149:6*). Prayer is made for one thing at a time until they have resisted the gates and they are broken. Then they receive the promise in their spirit that it is done.

Matthew 18:19:   It shall be done for them of my Father which is in Heaven.

KNOW YOUR ENEMY: SATAN

SECTION FOUR (A)

I. SATAN'S CREATED PURPOSE - EZEKIEL 28

A. Satan began as the angel Lucifer, a cherub.
   1. Many theologians believe that three archangels (or princes), exist. Only Michael, however, is named, *(Daniel 10:13)*.
       a. Michael, they believe, served with God and was the prince of Israel, *(Daniel 12:1)*.
       b. Gabriel serves the Holy Spirit and stands before God, *(Luke 1:19)*.
       c. Haleo, (or Lucifer), served with Jesus, *(Ezekiel. 28:11-17)*.
   2. Angels play a crucial part in carrying out God's plan in heaven.
   3. Angels are God's ministers in heaven. They have specific tasks assigned to them.
       a. Cherubim *(Ezekiel 28:14)*
       b. Seraphim *(Isaiah 6:2)*
       c. Angels
           They are ministering spirits, *(Hebrews 1:14)*.
           They have charge over us, *(Psalm 91:11)*.
           They perform miracles, *(Acts 5:19, 12:7,8)*.
           They minister judgment, *(Revelation 16:1)*.
           They minister revelation, *(Hebrews 2:2)*.
   4. Lucifer was created for the specific purpose of serving, (ministering).

B. Lucifer was the forerunner. Some believe he was probably used in the creation of other angels.
   1. He was the anointed cherub (given power) that covereth, *(Ezek. 28:14)*.
   2. He was anointed for a lay leadership position among the other angels.
   3. He occupied the position of "chief of staff" before his rebellion.

   Note: The rebellion of Satan has been compared to the saying, "The music minister wanted to become the senior pastor."

   4. As a created being, his power is limited, *(Job 1,2)*.

C. Lucifer was Christ's highest creation at that point in time, *(Ezekiel 28:12)*.
   1. He "sealed up the sum."
   2. He was full of wisdom.
   3. He was perfect in beauty.
   4. The throne room of God was available to him.
       a. He was made to be like God-not to be God.
       b. Because of his pride, Satan lost sight of the fact that he was a created being.
   5. He walked in the garden.
   6. He had a covering, *(v.13)*.
   7. The voice of Lucifer was pleasing to God.
   8. He led the Angels in praise before the throne.

II. LUCIFER REBELLED AGAINST GOD AND LOST HIS POSITION IN HEAVEN.

Revelation 12:9 "And the huge dragon was cast down and out, that ages-old serpent, who is called the Devil and Satan, he who is the seducer (deceiver) of all humanity the world over; he was forced out and down to the earth, and his angels were flung out along with him."

A. He was cast to this earth.

B. He, and 1/3 of heaven's angels, (now demons) were cast down with him.

III. LUCIFER FELL, (LOST HIS POSITION WITH GOD), BECAUSE OF HIS PRIDE. THE "MULTITUDE OF MERCHANDISE" IS PRIDE (*EZEKIEL 28:15-16*).

A. He lost sight of his created position as a servant.

B. His heart was lifted up because of his beauty.

C. He lost sight of the fact that everything he was came from God - his wisdom, authority, anointing, and life.

D. He desired to be worshipped, *"I will be like the most High."*

IV. SATAN'S FIVE "I WILLS" (*ISAIAH 14:12-17*)

A. *I will ascend into heaven.*

B. *I will exalt my throne about the stars of God,* (above the angels).

C. *I will sit also upon the mount of congregation...* (the throne room of God).

D. *I will ascend above the heights of the clouds.*

E. *I will be like the Most High,* (the absolute authority).
   1. "I will be like God."
   2. "I will not serve - I will be served."
   3. A sign of satan's control of your life is that you also disire to be your own god.

V. SATAN'S DIFFERENT IDENTITIES

A. Angel of light *II Corinthians 11:14*

B. Adversary *I Peter 5:8*

C. Tempter *I Thessalonians 3:5*

D. Deceiver *II Corinthians 11:3, Revelation 12:9, 13:14*

E. Hinderer *I Thessalonians 2:18*

F. Beast *Revelation 19:19*

G. God of the world *II Corinthians 4:4*

H. Prince of the power of the air *Ephesians 2:2*

Test all doctrine. The Bible is a test. It is not a way of proving a position. You test your doctrine against God's Word. If it does not stand, change it to the truth of the Word. Many will take a scripture and build a doctrine. This must not be done. Take all scripture in the light of its text - Chapter and verse. DON'T DWELL ON SATAN OR DEMONOLOGY - PURSUE JESUS! *"Greater is He that is in us than he that is in the world,"* *(I John 4:4)*.

Know your enemy that you can recognize him in the Light (prayer). You can't see him in the dark (life without prayer).

VI. SATAN'S DESTINY

A. Satan is already under a death sentence, *(I Cor. 2:7-8)*.
  1. He will be cast into hell for torment for eternity.
  2. Hell itself was specifically designed for satan and his angels.
  3. To enter hell a person must deny the cross.

B. Someday at the Great White Throne Judgment you will see satan, *(Isaiah 14:16)*.
  1. He will take on the form of a man.
  2. You will be amazed.
     a. *"Is this a man..."* (that made the earth to tremble?)
     b. He will not appear the fearsome creature you believe him to be.
  3. Satan is a totally defeated foe.
  4. You as Christian need to appropriate totally this victory into your life.
     a. You walk in victory as you pursue Jesus.
     b. You are victorious over satan in high praise to Jesus, *(Psalm 149:6-9)*.
  5. You cannot defeat satan in your own strength.

C. You can also maintain your walk by "keeping short accounts" and by dealing with sin in your life quickly, *(I John 1:9)*.

I. THE CHRISTIAN'S SPIRITUAL WARFARE AND VICTORY

A. Since the fall of satan, you must choose between two masters.
1. One master is your flesh.
   a. The flesh is always based on pride.
   b. The flesh is always in agreement with the enemy.
   c. Religion is the activity of the flesh.
2. The other master is the Holy Spirit.
   a. Brokenness is the "good soil" of which Jesus spoke.
   b. Brokenness is the opposite of pride.
   c. Proud persons do not pursue Jesus, *Galatians 5:17; "For the desires of the flesh are opposed to the (Holy) Spirit, and the [desires of the] Spirit are opposed to the flesh (Godless human nature); for these are antagonistic to each other - continually withstanding and in conflict with each other - so that you are not free but are prevented from doing what you desire to do." (Amplified)*

B. The Christian has as much resistance to satan as he has submission to Christ. *James 4:7 "so be subject to God - Stand firm against the devil; resist him and he will flee from you." (Amplified)*

C. Understand that satan is not omnipresent, *(Ephesians 6:12).*
1. He is one individual.
2. He has a chain of command under him.

D. Also, Satan will not release a person from bondage, *(Isaiah 14:17).*
1. You must take authority over him to overcome him.
2. Sometimes a demon can be cast out of a man.
3. Sometimes only prayer and fasting can cast out a demon.
4. You must pray daily (since prayer is the battlefield) for the release and freedom of those in bondage.

II. YOU HAVE A RIGHT TO BIND THE "STRONG MAN"

A. *Matthew 12:29*
It is not you but it is the Holy Spirit that binds...

If you are going to enter the realm of warfare praying...

1. You must be aware that a Christian who has not experienced deliverance but engages in the warfare of deliverance for someone else many times will create problems in his own life.
2. You must first be delivered from the bondage in your own life.
3. As the Bible tells you to "stand," it speaks of an offensive, attacking posture.

4. The Christian who has been delivered enters into a new realm of activity.
5. If there is someone whom you want to see delivered, saved, or freed, begin to pray to bind satan from his life.
6. Persons are "jailed" or "incarcerated" in satan's prison. They cannot escape and satan will not release them, *(Isaiah 14:17)*. They must be broken out.
7. Prayer is warfare - standing against the enemy in a circumstance of a person's life.
   a. You pray through to release, *(Luke 18:1)*.
   b. At that point, the enemy no longer can influence that circumstance until ground is given again. If possible teach that person to stand.
   c. Remember, the enemy is arrested only through a Christian's prayers, *(Matthew 12:28,29)*.

B. Again, over an entire nation is a prince and principality of demons, *(Daniel 10:2-21 Amp.)*.
1. Sometimes you can walk into a room in your house and sense an uneasiness.
   a. Demon oppression may be in that room.
   b. Purging of certain occultic or satanic objects, (for example, pictures or objects of those things called unclean in Scripture: rock music posters, toys, games, etc.) will be expedient to clear the oppression.
   c. Demons can house themselves in statuary.

C. Demonic forces are set up in a governmental structure.
1. There is a chain of command of demonic forces, *(Ephesians 6:12)*.
2. There exists a "prince demon" assigned over each nation, city, etc. The person that has demons will always have a prince in charge, such as found in *Mark 5:6,7* the one who spoke for the Legion.
3. These subservient demons take orders handed down through the hierarchy just as a military man takes orders from his commanding officer. (Princes, principalities, powers) - spiritual wickedness in high places. There are four known echelons of demonic structure.

D. Entire cities can be changed as Christians pray to bind the prince from over his principality, *(Daniel 10:20,21)*.
1. You must understand who you are in Jesus.
2. You, as a Christian, have the authority to drive the enemy from the camp.
3. You need to "bind the strongman and spoil his goods."
4. You do this by going to God in the Name of Jesus Christ and by faith bringing all that He stands for against the stronghold. It then will come down.

E. Christians can pray to bind the devil from the affairs of the lost person, (tares planted among the wheat), who may even be in a position of authority in a local fellowship. That lost person will be thwarted and confused in his/her attempts to disturb the church.
1. Satan will place a prince in the church to fight several things, three of which are...
   a. The deeper teachings of the Christ-filled life
   b. Pastoral authority thereby binding the spiritual leader
   c. Most importantly, true prayer in the church
2. Revival can come to a body of saints only by broken people praying, (entering into warfare), to bind the enemy - ALL PRAYER IS WARFARE.
3. Make sure of your own right standing with God before you enter into warfare.

F. Remember, to insure God's hand upon your life during the day, pray this prayer each morning: "Lord, I agree with you for what is written in Heaven for my life today." Then continue to praise until you have knowledge that the peace is there, *(Jer. 33:3).*
   1. This is a position of agreement with God that the bondage satan would introduce in your life is broken.
   2. According to *Ephesians 2:10 and Psalm 139:16,* every day of a believers's life is already established by the Lord: *"For we are God's (own) handiwork (His workmanship), recreated in Christ Jesus, (born anew) that we may do those good works which God predestined (planned beforehand) for us, (taking paths which He prepared ahead of time) that we should walk in them - living the good life which He prearranged and made ready for us to live." (Amp.)*
   3. Stay with it in Praise until you experience peace. When you have the knowledge of peace, you have transferred ownership of your life back to Christ for the day.

ONCE COMMITTED AND RECEIVED IN SPIRIT BY CHRIST THEN YOU BECOME A WEAPON IN THE HANDS OF GOD BY VIRTUE OF WALKING IN THE SPIRIT. HERE ARE THE RESULTS...

G. *Luke 11:22 "But when one stronger than he attacks him and conquers him, he robs him of his whole armor on which he had relied, and divides up and distributes all his goods as plunder (spoil)." (Amp.)*
   1. Satan's main ploy, (especially in the family), is to divide.
   2. For example, if he can get a husband or wife to quarrel and each one go off on his/her respective "tangents," the devil wins a great victory.
   3. Likewise, he desires the Christian to be unforgiving, *(II Corinthians 2:10,11).*
   4. Your position is to be offensive. You are to be aggressive toward satan in the Name of Jesus Christ.

H. Persons who enter into a deliverance ministry are often outcasts. Are you willing to pay the price to go on with God?
   1. People often have "pet sins" they are not willing to give up. "Spirit filled" Christians anger them.
   2. If they do not forsake those pet sins they cannot go on for God.
   3. When a Christian brother stands against the stronghold, conflict and conviction is brought into the person's life for which he is praying.
   4. The tares, (people planted by satan), will come against him in violence.
      Some statements that are often made are...
      ⇒ they are not Baptists...
      ⇒ they are not Methodists...
      ⇒ they have gone off the deep end...
      ⇒ Charismatics don't believe that way...
      ⇒ etc....

I. *Luke 10:17 "The seventy returned with joy, saying, Lord, even the demons are subject to us in Your name!"*
   1. They bound the "strong man and spoiled his goods."
   2. They used the name of Jesus in authority.
   3. In *Luke 10:18*, Jesus is referring to satan being cast out of Heaven by the spoken word.
   4. In the same way, as these disciples spoke the name of Jesus they "bound the strongman and spoiled his goods," (spoiled means "to take away from").

J. *Mark 3:27 "But no one can go into a strong man's house and ransack his household goods right and left and seize them as plunder, unless he first binds the strong man; then indeed he may [thoroughly] plunder his house." (Amplified)*
   1. In order to bind the strongman you must be in right standing with God yourself.
   2. You must be delivered from the strongholds in your own life before you can assume the offensive position and tear down strongholds in another's life.

III. SATAN IS ALREADY DEFEATED.

A. The blood of Christ has defeated him.

B. The Word of Faith has defeated him. *Revelation 12:11: "And they have overcome (conquered) him by means of the blood of the Lamb and by the utterance of their testimony, for they did not love and cling to life even when faced with death - holding their lives cheap till thy had to die [for their witnessing]." (Amplified)*

IV. THE BREAKING OF THE BONDAGE IN YOUR LIFE BEGINS WHEN YOU ARE BORN AGAIN.

The beginning of deliverance is salvation.

V. JESUS IS LIGHT

A. As you pursue Him you walk in the light.

B. As you walk in His light you overcome darkness, *(John 8:12, John 9:5, Matthew 5:14).*

WHAT ARE THE SIGNS OF DEMON POSSESSION? THE CLASSIC SIGNS BIBLICALLY ARE FOUND IN *MARK 5:1-19*.

I.   FACTS ABOUT THE DEMONIAC

A. He was demented.

B. He was not a mental case but a "demon case."
   1. He suffered not from psychological disorder.
   2. He was acting as the demons in him dictated.

C. He lived among the dead.

D. Satan, who hates man because he is made in the image of God, degrades him as much as he can.

II.   SIGNS OF DEMON POSSESSION

The Constant Presence of Death

A. People who are demonized or demon possessed have an affinity for death.
   1. They are forced to dwell on death in every form:
      a. Rock music
      b. Movies
      c. Games
      d. Toys
   2. They talk often about their own death, *(John 8:44)*.
   3. Suicide is a demon-controlled event.
   4. In watching the movies about death and dwelling on death, the demon possessed man appeases the demons in him.
   5. Satan operates in death. Jesus brings life.

Great Physical Strength

B. People who are demon possessed have great physical strength.
   1. In asylums, often times the inmates will have superhuman strength.
      a. The man himself is not all that strong.
      b. The demons who are dwelling in him supply the strength.
   2. The bondage in a person's life can only be broken by another's prayer for him.
      a. Even a very softly spoken prayer can stir up the demons.
      b. Every demon must bow at the name of Jesus, *(Philippians 2:10)*.
      c. Prayer, using the name of Jesus in authority, by the Spirit, will break demonic bondage.
   3. Just like the demoniac in *Mark 5,* a demon-possessed man can scarcely be restrained.

Restless - Never At Peace

C. Demon-possessed people are restless.
   1. The man in *Mark 5* wandered.
   2. These people are never at rest.
   3. They are hyperactive.
   4. They have a drive to take drugs or drink or to submit to rock music.
      a. The demons are in control and are demanding satisfaction.
      b. Demons are always in agreement with the flesh.

Nakedness

D. Nakedness is a sign of demon possession.
   1. Homosexuality (a manifestation of demon possession) seeks to expose all the flesh possible and to make all sexual activity open and public.
   2. Demons can prey on a person's lust to expose flesh.
   3. Pornography, pedophilia, fornication, adultery... Lust out of control is spirit. (There are two outside spirits: the Holy Spirit, including angels as ministering spirits, and the unholy spirit.)

Attacking Of Their Own Flesh

E. Self-mutilation is a sign of demon possession.
   1. Man is created in God's image.
   2. Satan, who hates man does all he can do to destroy the human body.
      a. Tattoos
      b. Bash-dancing or Slam-dancing of punk rockers
      c. Drugs, alcohol, food, coffee, etc.
      d. Self-inflicted wounds

F. Demon possessed people or demonized Christians have a death wish.
   1. Suicide
   2. drawn to Rock Music by the beat
   3. Games - dungeons and dragons - toys of death, demonic cartoons or movies

III. NOW HOW DID THE STORY END?

A. The man recognized Jesus.
   1. He recognized Jesus as the Son of God.
   2. He acknowledged Jesus as having authority over demons.

B. He fell at Jesus' feet and worshipped Him.

C. Jesus spoke to a single demon in him, *"...what is your name..."*
   1. Jesus addressed the "prince demon," (the man had a legion - at least 1700 demons in him under a prince named Legion)
   2. Jesus discerned the demon in command and dealt with that demon.

D. The prince demon replied to Jesus.
   1. Legion knew who Jesus was.
   2. The demon knew Jesus as the Son of God, with all power over the enemy.
   3. They could not leave without Christ's permission.

E. When Jesus allowed them to go into the swine the demon possessed man was delivered.
   1. He appropriated the victory by taking authority over the demon, by confessing Jesus, and by presenting himself to Him.
   2. He won by pursuing Jesus.
   3. All can be free when they move toward the Light, (Jesus Christ).

F. You as a Christian can likewise take authority over demons in the name of Jesus. You present Light when you pray, thereby dispelling darkness.

G. The townspeople came, *(Mark 5:15),* and witnessed the man clothed and in his right mind.

IV. THESE THINGS HAPPENED TO THE MAN AFTER HE HAD BEEN DELIVERED

A. "He was sitting."
   1. The restlessness was gone.
   2. He was at peace.

B. "He was clothed."
   1. He no longer wanted to expose himself.
   2. His deliverance brought modesty.

C. "He was in his 'right mind.'"

D. "He became a witness for Jesus."
   1. He was free to testify.
   2. He was freed by Jesus and was quick to acknowledge from where his liberty came, *(Mark 5:18).*

V. STEPS FOR PERSONAL DELIVERANCE

A. Prayerfully compile a list of all the unconfessed sins in your life.

B. Confess each sin aloud to God. Confess means to agree with God that these are sins of which you should stand convicted. In doing this you take power away from satan and break the bondage.

C. Appropriate the cleansing that is now yours by confessing, "Lord I receive forgiveness and cleansing of (name of specific sin). Thank you for forgiving me for (specific sin). Your blood cleanses me from (specific sin). I receive it now." One must only confess a sin once to be forgiven of it if it is asked in brokenness and seriousness.

D. Speak aloud to satan using the Name of Jesus in authority and verbally break any contacts you have made with him as regards this sin, *(Matthew 4).* Follow these steps for each sin on your list. At that point, praise the Lord. You are set free of any guilt and free of any grip satan would have on you.

E. Destroy the list. As the sin has been destroyed, so destroy the memory of it. Put it under the Blood.
   1. *Psalm 103:12*
   2. *Micah 7:19*
   3. *Isaiah 44:22*
   4. *I John 1:9*

F. Any future accusations of satan should be quickly taken through this procedure. In doing so you actually use satan's attacks on you against him!! Say: "The Blood of Jesus Christ cleanses me from all sin!" Begin to Praise the Lord in the matter - for Praise is a sword of <u>Offense</u>.

G. Give Jesus possession of everything in your life.
   Examples:
   1. Things
   2. Position: say "Jesus, you be the Father, Mother, Husband, Wife, Pastor, Elder, deacon, Christian, Businessman you want to be through me."
   3. Positively confess, "I am crucified with Christ. Jesus you are the Lord of my life. I am filled with the Holy Spirit," and begin to Praise the Lord.

H. Pray
   "Lord, I agree with you for what is written in Heaven for my life today. I claim *Ephesians 2:10 and Psalm 139:16* for my life." Praise Him seven times a day! Say in your mind, "Lord Jesus, I love you." Quote Scripture in your mind over and over as you go to sleep. Remember, you are already free indeed. But you must go after it!

THE FIVE U'S OF UNANSWERED PRAYER

Beloved,

This message contains the Five U's of Unanswered Prayer. It is my belief that these five U's are presented in the order by which you hear from God. Prayerfully test yourself at each place before you go on. Remember, the only sign of spiritual maturity is answered prayer.

Mickey

You must begin at the beginning. Have you been to Calvary?

I. **IN ORDER TO HEAR, YOU MUST BE BORN AGAIN.**

The moment you are saved your body becomes the Temple of God. The Holy Spirit comes to dwell within you, complete with the Mind of Christ as well as God's Will for you.

A. Jesus' Prayers were always heard and answered because satan had nothing in Him, *(John 14:30)*.

> *14:30 Hereafter I will not talk much with you: for the prince of this world cometh, and hath nothing in me.*

1. No strongholds
2. No sin
3. No unforgiveness
4. He could hear from the Father, and agree with the Father's Will.

Jesus Christ prayed to the Father. When He prayed to the Father, the Father spoke His mind to the Son. Jesus confessed the mind of the Father, by Faith, and the blind saw, the lame walked, the dead came to life. Everything Jesus did... He did by the Power of the Father through Him.

CHRIST'S POWER WAS GOD THROUGH HIM.

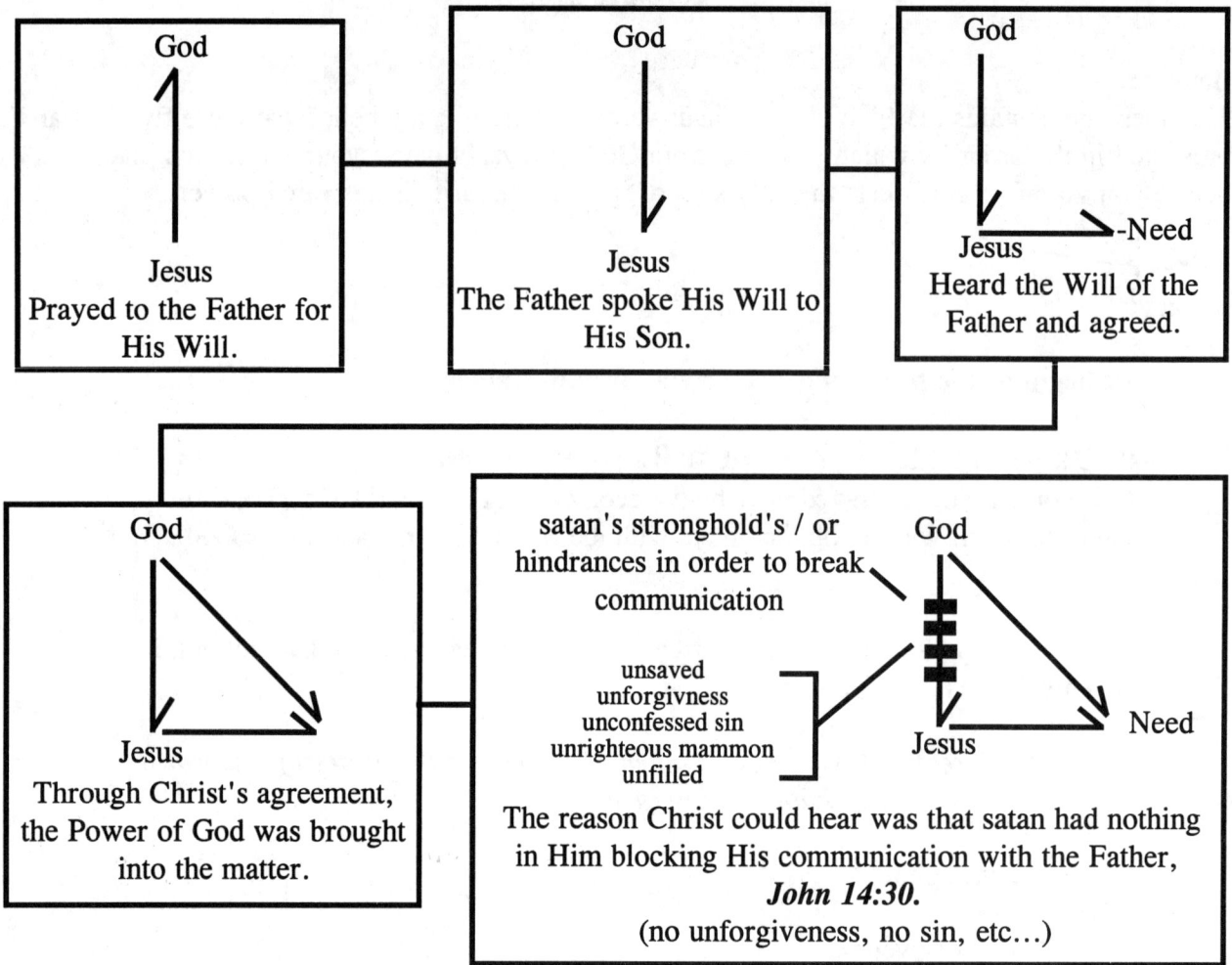

The key to praying is hearing... *John 5:17, 19, 30*. As Jesus heard from the Father he agreed and the Father moved in. The reason that Christ could hear from the Father was because Satan had nothing in Christ - no strongholds. The devil could not hinder Christ from hearing from the Father.

B. God speaks His mind, but most can't hear because of sin in their lives.

C. Praise tears down strongholds, *(James 1:2-4, Psalm 149:6-9, II Corinthians 10:3-5).*

D. God does not hear the prayers of a sinner, (the Greek word for hear is "akovo" which means "give audience to," *John 9:31).*
   1. He does not hear a lost man, except in the cry to be born again, *(Romans 10:9,10).*
   2. He does not hear a carnal Christian, except in the cry to be forgiven, *(John 9:31, I John 1:9).*

E. You must be born from above.
1. God draws you to Himself. He will not come to you when you think you are ready to be saved, *(John 6:44)*.
2. The Holy Spirit convicts the unregenerate of sin and by deep conviction draws the sinner to Jesus Christ for salvation.
3. The sinner, now aware he/she is not only lost and facing judgment, but also aware that he/she is helpless to correct this situation, responds to the effectual wooing of the Holy Spirit and gives his life to Christ.
4. If you were not broken over your sin, you were not born again. (That is to say, if you made a decision without conviction then there was very likely no conversion.) When the Holy Spirit reveals to you your sins, you will be convicted. For instance, if you just shook the preacher's hand and said, "Pastor, my wife seems to think I ought to get baptized and join the church," you did not leave the building adopted, (or as an "Engrafted branch"). Without conviction, there is no true repentance and conversion.
5. You must be saved in order to worship Him in the Spirit.
   a. You received all of the Holy Spirit you are ever going to get when you were saved. The object from there is that the Holy Spirit gets all of you, *(Ephesians 5:18)*.
   b. You must give yourself fully to Jesus Christ. Does He have all of you?

To understand the truth of this is to realize that you must be saved to experience true worship. The Scripture says in *Philippians 3:3a "for we [Christians] are the true circumcision, who worship God in the spirit and by the Spirit of God..." (Amplified)* The spirit dwells only in the born again believer and communes with the Father. That is true worship.

The person who has no remorse over his/her sins is not being dealt with by the Holy Spirit. Therefore there is no conviction and no real repentance.

Satan, in order to keep the Christian from hearing from God, (*"Thy Kingdom come, Thy Will be done on earth as it is in heaven,"*) places a stronghold, a gate of hell, in the Christian's life to keep him from hearing from the Will of God to agree.
Satan fights your hearing. Again, you go to God in the Name of Jesus, bringing all that you believe about that name. He comes back to you with His mind, the mind of the Father brought through His Son's ministry that Christ had with the Father. It is still the Father's Will.

II.   UNFORGIVENESS BLOCKS ANSWERED PRAYER AND THE HEARING OF GOD'S WILL.

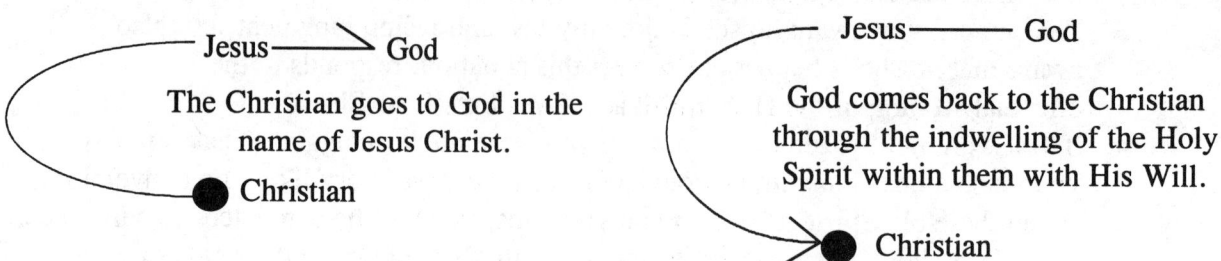

Jesus ——→ God

The Christian goes to God in the
name of Jesus Christ.

● Christian

Jesus —— God

God comes back to the Christian
through the indwelling of the Holy
Spirit within them with His Will.

● Christian

**SATAN THEN MOVES INTO THE LIFE OF THE BELIEVER WITH GATES, WALLS, FORTIFIED
CASTLES, TO BLOCK THE WILL OF GOD**

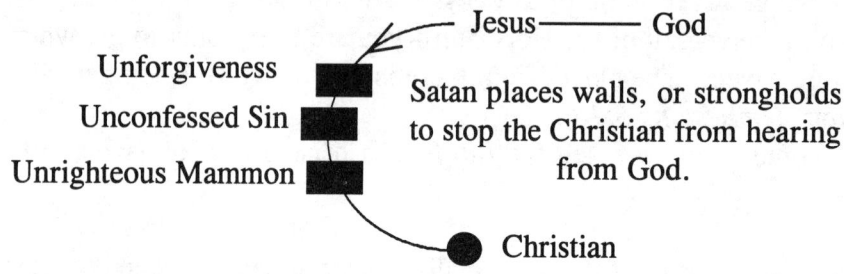

Unforgiveness

Unconfessed Sin

Unrighteous Mammon

Jesus —— God

Satan places walls, or strongholds
to stop the Christian from hearing
from God.

● Christian

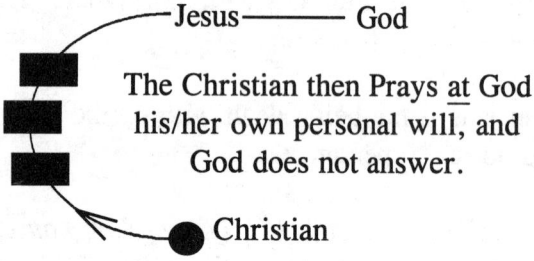

Jesus —— God

The Christian then Prays <u>at</u> God
his/her own personal will, and
God does not answer.

● Christian

A. God works in your present and future, *(Ephesians 2:10),* while the enemy works out of
your past, *(Phil. 3:13).*

B. If there is some event out of your past that you cannot talk objectively and
dispassionately about, you have a stronghold, *(II Corinthians 10:3-6).*
1. Satan has engineered this unresolved issue in your life to prevent you from
hearing from God.
2. The issue must be resolved on the basis of praise before you can go on with God.

If you have anything in your heart against someone, living or dead, not one prayer you pray is answered. If you cannot talk about negative events without getting emotional you have a stronghold.

C. If you say you walk with God (with some attendant gift) and court bitterness against anyone, saved or lost, dead or alive, God's Word says you are in darkness, (and your "gift" is probably <u>false</u>), *(II Corinthians 11:4)*.
1. At this point, you do not hear from God.

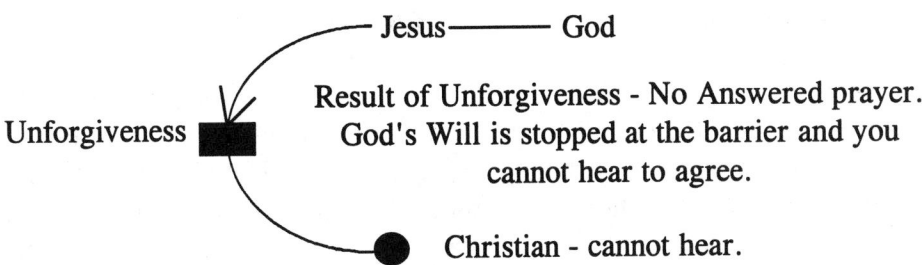

Jesus ———— God

Result of Unforgiveness - No Answered prayer.
God's Will is stopped at the barrier and you
cannot hear to agree.

Unforgiveness

Christian - cannot hear.

2. At this point, you don't have a ministry.
3. At this point, you are no threat to satan because you have been ensnared by him.
4. Therefore you must resort to religion (ministry in the flesh).

Christians Must Forgive Christians.

If you have anything in your heart against another Christian, God says in *I John 2:8* that your sins are not forgiven and you do not walk in the light. *I John 2:9-11*, states ***"if you say you are in the light and hate your brother (Christian) you are in darkness."*** You are never to ask a believer with unforgiveness to pray for you. Nor are you to receive instruction from this person because he does not hear from God. Satan has consumed his "walk" with God through bitterness, *(Ephesians 4:31, Hebrews 12:15)*.

D. *I John 4:20*, If you say you love God and yet (actually) hate your brother (Christian), you are a *"liar."*
1. If you hold something against a fellow born again believer, you walk in darkness.
2. God's love, or Will, does not flow through an unforgiving heart.
3. God still loves you. You, however, do not love God, (by His own words.)

You are blinded in darkness... God's love may be in you but it is bottled up within you by satan.

Q. What is your price to know God?
A. Forgive those who have trespassed against you, *(Matthew 18:35)*.

Matthew 6:14,15

14 For if you forgive people their trespasses - that is, their <u>reckless</u> and <u>willful</u> sins, leaving them, letting them go and giving up resentment - your heavenly Father will also forgive you.

15 But if you do not forgive others their trespasses - their reckless and willful sins, leaving them, letting them go and giving up resentment - neither will your Father forgive you your trespasses. (Amplified)

E. You are to forgive *Reckless Sins.*

For example - Recently a man in a drunken condition got into his pickup truck. In a state of inebriation he became disoriented, entered an exit ramp on a freeway, crashed headlong into a church bus and killed 27 people - 17 of which were children. If those families walk with God what are they to do to the drunk man that caused the crash? FORGIVE.

F. You are also to forgive *Willful Sins.*

1. **For example** - A woman left her infant child with her mother to go shopping. Upon her return she found her mother murdered. She went looking for her baby, and it too was slain. Then, nine months later her husband asked for a divorce because he could not stand the pain any longer. She asked the question "Are you telling me I am to forgive?" The answer - "What is your price?" She praised through until she received peace in each event. She forgave and God used her wonderfully in a Prayer Ministry.

You are to forgive *"reckless, and willfull"* sins, *(Matthew 6:14,15).*

2. You must forgive the lost as well as the saved.
3. If there is anything out of your past that you cannot forgive, you are impotent in the Kingdom of God.
4. What is your Price?

G. If you do not forgive, your Father will not hear your prayers.
1. Bitterness equals immaturity.
2. No resentment is worth unanswered prayer, being that God has made a way of escape.

H. The giving of offerings to God from an unforgiving heart is unacceptable, *(Matthew 5:23, 24).* The Christian remembering that another Christian has ought against him must make resolution. If this is not done the gift will not carry the blessing of God back to the giver. Many will attempt to operate in the promise *"give and it shall be given unto you" (Luke 6:38),* but it does not work. They give, but get no response from God. Unforgiveness is very likely the reason.

   1. You must forgive.
   2. Forgiveness precedes giving.
   3. Even giving is warfare, when done by revelation. But you must be able to hear from God. <u>Unforgiveness stops the hearing.</u>

NO HEARING, NO AGREEING. NO AGREEING, NO ANSWERED PRAYER.

I. Who are you to hold something against someone else after you have been forgiven so much? *(Matthew 18:2-35)*

   1. Jesus has forgiven you of so much.
   2. You have trouble forgiving others of small transgressions.
   3. This type of unforgiving will lead to demonization of a Christian. Jesus gives a classic example of how demons enter the flesh of the Christian. A king has a servant who owed him the equivilent of 10 million dollars. He called for the debt to be paid. The servant could not pay and begged his Master for patience. His Master was so moved with compassion he forgave and totally released the debt. Later, the forgiven servant (salvation) met another slave that owed him the equivilent of 10 dollars and demanded his money by grabbing him by the throat *(18:28).* He wanted payment. The *"fellow servant fell down at his feet"* and begged for the same patience that was granted to the first servant. He would not forgive the 10 dollar debt and cast him in to the debtor's prison till he could pay the debt. Other servants heard of the situation and sought the king to tell what had been done. The king called for the first servant, and said, *"thou wicked servant should you not have had compassion (forgiveness) on a fellow servant as I had <u>pity</u> on thee?"* He then delivered him to the tormentors (demons) till he could pay...

Demons enter the Christian's flesh through the door of unforgiveness.

Your sins have been forgiven for His name sake. Who are you to hold sin in your life on the basis of unforgiveness?

Again, the way to tell that the stronghold is broken is when you can talk about the past event without becoming emotional about it, *(James 5:16).*

If there is any unforgiveness still in your past and you cannot praise God and get through it, then you are dead, neutered, and powerless as a weapon in the hands of God, and there is no glory of God manifested or moving in your life.

Give up your resentment - forgive, *(I Corinthians 2:10,11)*.

10 To whom ye forgive anything, I [forgive] also: for if I forgave anything, to whom I forgave [it], for your sakes [forgave I it] in the person of Christ;
11 Lest Satan should get an advantage of us: for we are not ignorant of his devices.

Here you are commanded forgiveness in the Name of Christ. You are to attack memory in Praise until forgiveness by the Blood has blotted out the hate or resentment. This is done by forgiving in the Name of Jesus Christ. When this is done the power of demon forces are broken in the believer.

Verse 11 states that if it there is not forgivness then satan has the *"advantage"* of you. This means control of your prayer life. He destroys the power to and through you.

To not forgive makes you ignorant, (Greek word "agnoeho" which means - "ignore - through lack of information or intelligence"), of his devices, (Greek word "noema" which means "purposes"). Satan must make you hate. Then, when you have unforgivness, your power and purpose in Christ is destroyed, *(Ephesians 2:10)*.

What Is Your Price???

Psalm 66:18 If I regard Inquity, (know I have unconfessed sin in my life), God will not hear me.

Isa. 59:2 But your inquities (unforgiveness) have separated between you and your God and your sins have hid His face (His Will) from you that He will not hear.

KEY to hearing from God = Forgiveness

Q. Is holding on to resentment and unforgiveness greater to you than a relationship with God?
A. No, it doesn't matter what has happened to you, present or past! God's Grace is sufficient.

Q. What is your price to go on with God?

III. **UNCONFESSED SIN BLOCKS PRAYER, (ANYTHING THAT YOU HAVE NOT DEALT WITH IN BROKENNESS). SIN CONFESSED WITHOUT CONVICTION IS NOT TRUE REPENTANCE.**

A. *Be sure your sin will find you out, (Num. 32:23).*
1. If you cover your sins, you will not prosper.
2. The entire human race fell as a result of one man's sin, *(Romans 5:12).*

B. An unregenerate man always commits sin.
1. Sin is genetic. You are born as a sinner. The race fell with Adam's Sin.
2. You are conceived in sin, *(Psalm 51:5).*
3. The mind is defiled (darkness), *(Titus 1:15).*
4. The heart is wicked - evil thoughts, *(Mark 7:21).*
5. The flesh is corrupt, (Greek = human nature), *(Romans 7:18).*
6. The unsaved always seek after that which satisfies the flesh, *(Romans 8:1,5).*
7. To be carnally minded is death, *(Romans 8:6).*
8. The carnal mind is "hostile" toward God, *(Romans 8:6).*
   a. "Enmity" equals "hostile." The carnal Christian is in opposition to any real move of the Holy Spirit.
   b. These verses also apply to the backslidden Christian.

If you have unconfessed sin in your life, be sure your sin will find you out, *(Numbers 32:23).*

If there is still no breakthrough when you get to the point that you have forgiven all and confessed all - Pray, "Lord what is it in my life that I cannot remember or that I cannot sense?" Ask the Lord to reveal it to you so that you can deal with it. He will not give you stone for bread. He will tell you.

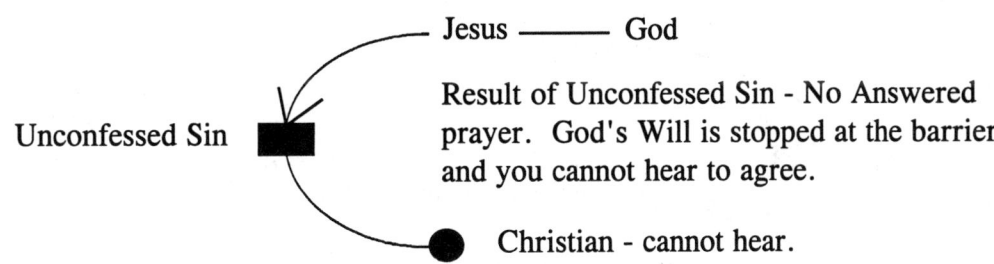

Jesus ——— God

Result of Unconfessed Sin - No Answered prayer. God's Will is stopped at the barrier and you cannot hear to agree.

Unconfessed Sin

Christian - cannot hear.

IV. UNRIGHTEOUS MAMMON BLOCKS PRAYER.

Luke 16:11 Therefore, if you have not been faithful in the [case of] the unrighteous mammon -- the deceitful riches, money, possessions -- who will entrust to you the true riches? (Amp.)

A. Mammon is money, (possessions), *(Luke 16:11)*.
   1. Unrighteous mammon deals with stored or horded wealth. Example: the Israelites could not store the mammon of the Old Testament. In the New Testament the man who built bigger barns was judged, *(Luke 12:18)*.
   2. Christians are to be a stream, not a dam, *(Luke 6:38)*.
   3. Nowhere in scripture are you as an individual told to store wealth, *(Prov. 11:24, II Cor. 9:6)*.

B. *"True riches"* are the mind of God.
   1. The mind of God is already settled. You cannot change the mind of God.
   2. You can find the mind of God through prayer and then agree with it, *(Phil. 2:5, Rom. 12:1-2, John 15:7)*.

C. In order for God to entrust the mind of Christ *("True Riches")* to a beliver, He must first be able to trust the believer with mammon. This trust is built as the Christian returns all back to the Lord. Transfers ownership, tithes, and gives by revelation.

   Again, *"True Riches"* = the mind of Christ = the keys to the Kingdom = *"Thy Kingdom come, Thy will be done on earth as it is in Heaven."*

   Q. If I have not been faithful in my mammon, I will not recieve the mind of Christ?
   A. That's Right!!!

D. You do not own anything. It all belongs to God. You are a steward, *(I Peter 4:10, I Cor. 4:1)*.

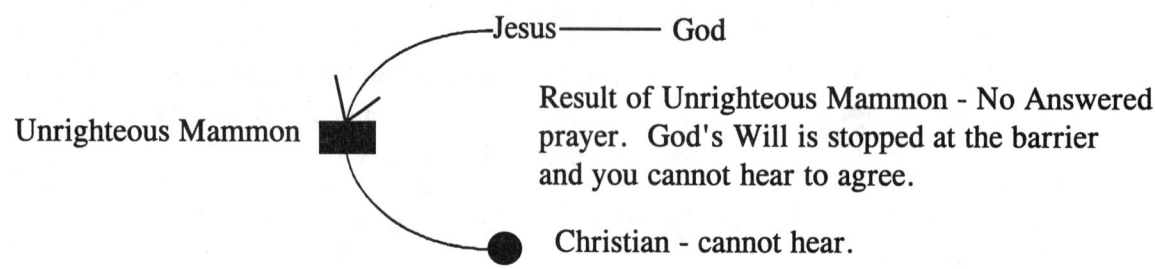

Jesus———— God

Unrighteous Mammon

Result of Unrighteous Mammon - No Answered prayer. God's Will is stopped at the barrier and you cannot hear to agree.

Christian - cannot hear.

E. Again, if you are not faithful to God in your finances, you will never find the mind of Christ.

F. You are Living at the coming of the Lord Jesus.
   1. One - World government is near.
   2. One - World banking is near.
   3. The system by which you now live will end.

G. How can you be faithful in your finances?
   1. Tithe: First, give yourself to God and then unto others by the Will of God, *(II Cor. 8:5)*.
   2. You then give by revelation - or God's Will in giving through you, *(Luke 6:38)*.

If you belong to God and operate in His Will, He extends His ministry and Glory through you. This begins by being obedient to the tithe, a full 10% of your gross income, *(Mal 3:7-11)*. The tithe is the Lord's and He will gather it from the true born again believer either by his giving, or His taking it through chastisement. The Christian will tithe one way or another. Many say that the tithe is Old Testament law. However, Jesus did not come to replace the Law but to fulfull it. A Christian filled with the Holy Spirit will automatically be led to tithe. It is an evident sign of his place in God's Will.

Tithing is an act of warfare. Satan, as the hinderer, will do all the harm to you that he can. He will keep you in a lack-of-faith position so that nothing can be done through you in prayer. When you tithe in obedience to God, the devourer is rebuked. Tithing is a must for the Christian in Spiritual Warfare.

   3. Then, give everything you have back to God, (Transfer ownership).
   4. Find the mind of Christ in prayer.
   5. Give and keep your mouth shut. Let God get the Glory. If you do this He will find He can trust you to bring Glory to His name and He will do more through you, *(Matthew 6:3, Luke 6:38)*.
   6. God then meets every need.

Here is one of the most unique areas of giving in the Bible based on God's return for the faithful giving by revelation. In *II Corinthians 8* - Paul explained the needs of the Christian Jews to the church at Macedonia. They responded by first giving themselves to God and then to him by God's Will - Revelation giving. He then was sharing this miracle with the church in Corinth to break them into doing something by God's revelation, thereby overcoming their carnality. He shared the glorious outpouring of grace unlimited, favor, overwhelming blessing, that God poured back upon the Macedonians *(II Cor. 8:1)*. As he personally witnessed God's response, he shared a promise from God for those who tithe, (obedience and revelation giving). His promise is that *"every earthly blessing will come in abundance."* The reason for this is that when you have learned to give by revelation after the tithe, God will give to you so that you will be *"self sufficient - possessing enough to require no aid or support and furnished in abundance for every good work and charitable donation."* You will need no aid or support, *(II Cor. 9:8 Amp.)*. This is a must position for every Christian as you approach the end times and men's hearts begin to fail. It is warfare.

H. Unrighteous mammon is one of the greatest barriers to answered prayer. You either possess your possessions or they possess you.

As the world continues toward a one-world government and bank, there will be a move to stop crime. Society will see a cashless society emerge, and at some point, each person will be implanted with a number upon the forehead and the back of the hand. Though the Christian will be gone at that time this world will go into the beginnings of the tribulation. You cannot trust in mammon. You must trust in God to supply His needs through you. You must transfer ownership of all that you have and guard it by prayer, ready to give as He directs.

The Position is...

1. Tithe to your local church. Your tithe is an act of obedience.
   It must be understood again that the tithe is an act of obedience and has an obedience reward. Giving is the ministry of Grace or God's Will through you. The treasures you lay up in heaven are the gifts that are given after prayer by God's revelation, *(Matthew 6:19-21)*. What He does through you is sent on ahead.
2. Then give above the tithe by revelation of God. This gift is above your tithe.
3. At that point, God grants you "True Riches," or His Will in your life: "The kingdom of God."
4. True financial freedom is "Spirit Giving."
5. If you do not you will never know God's full position and calling for your life.

Transfer ownership to God. Give by Revelation. God will then fulfill His will as He fulfills your calling and needs.

V. UNFILLED - *EPHESIANS 5:18*

18 And be not drunk with wine, wherein is excess; but be filled with the Spirit;

Q. What does it mean to be filled?
A. The spirit empowers you for ministry.

A. You must be empowered in order to do ministry.
   1. Take your life and go after Christ with all of your heart.
   2. Pursue Jesus aggressively.
   3. Present yourself a living sacrifice.

B. The true gifts of the Spirit are Jesus Christ manifesting Himself through you by the Holy Spirit, *(Gal 5:22-25).*

C. What is your price to become a soldier of Christ?

Again, you are called...

1. A Soldier *II Timothy 2:3*
2. A Warrior *II Corinthians 10:4, II Timothy 1:18*
3. An Avenger *Psalm 18:47*
4. An Intercessor *Rom. 8:26*
5. An Ambassador *II Corinthians 5:20, Ephesians 6:20*

Q. Are you any of these?

D. *"...Be ye transformed by the renewing of your mind,"* (Rom. 12:2).

  1. You are brought into the armor of God piece by piece in sequence of growth.

  2. You don't put on the armor. It is put on you at the level of your constant growth as you pursue the Lord.

Q. Putting on the Armor of God is a Growth Process? *(Eph. 6:11-17)*

A. *Ephesians* is a book of growing in the Spirit. The word *"In"* is used 99 times in subject matter in this epistle, more than in any other book in the bible. The process of growth begins at new birth. You get all of Christ that you will ever get when you are born again. Therefore, you have access to the armor. As a baby in Christ, however, you are unaware of its presence and power. You must first understand that every piece of armor <u>is</u> Christ. When you were saved, the "gird" was placed on you. You were girded with Truth, *(John 14:6)*. Then, as you daily battle the flesh to go on past the "milk" of the word *(I Cor 3:1-3)*, you grow in grace through prayer and bible study. You then begin to develop the second piece: *the breastplate of righteousness*. This means "right-standing," or right where God is in you. As obedience to *Matthew 6:33* occurs, you continue to mature. God's plan or path *(Eph 2:10 Amp.)* forms in your life as your *"feet are shod,"* (Greek - "Podeo," to bind under one's feet) with *"the gospel"* message. In other words you are placed onto the path of God's Will and ministry through your life. Continuing on in growth, God then puts on you the *shield of faith.* In *Gal 2:20* we find *"we are to live by the faith of the Son of God."* So as you grow your faith increases as you have built up within you by the Holy Spirit, the faith and person of Christ. It is by this position that you walk by faith (His Will) and not by sight, thereby quenching all the fiery darts of the wicked one. As you continue to daily practice the presence of the Lord in sequence of growth, God places upon your head or mind the *"helmet of salvation."* This is the mind of Christ, *(Romans 12:1-2, Phil. 2:5)*. People want to go from new birth to the mind of Christ in an instant. It does not work that way. A newborn can only take milk. It is through the process of maturity that the diet changes to meat. The same is true in the Christian walk. There must be growth to understand the voice and language of God. There is a plan for the Christian life everyday and you are to work it out *(Eph. 2:10)*. Again this is God's plan for you, already written out in heaven. It is actually the mind of Christ doing His Will and Work in your life, *(I Cor. 2:16)*. At this sequence of growth you become aware of the "Truth" that is revealed in the inward parts, *(Ps. 51:6)*. From that position of power, knowing that Jesus Christ is the Word, *(John 1:1-2)*, God matures you and places into your hand the *"sword of the spirit."* To the carnal Christian who is girded about with Truth only (salvation) the sword is a defense mechanism. To the growing Christian it is a weapon of attack. When Jesus dealt with satan in the wilderness he attacked with the Word, *(Matt. 4:4)*. His statement was *"it is written."* Satan was defeated by the Living Word, (Jesus Christ). The same Word dwells in every born again Christian. Then the Word at this level becomes God's instrument of warfare through you, but only if you are maturing daily, *(II Peter 3:18)*. Every piece of armor is Jesus Christ coming through your life as you grow in grace and knowledge. From that dressed position you then enter the next step given in *Eph. 6:18:* prayer. You dress in Christ that you/He will defeat the enemy. Prayer is the battle ground. At this point you are a seasoned warrior; for ALL PRAYER IS WARFARE.

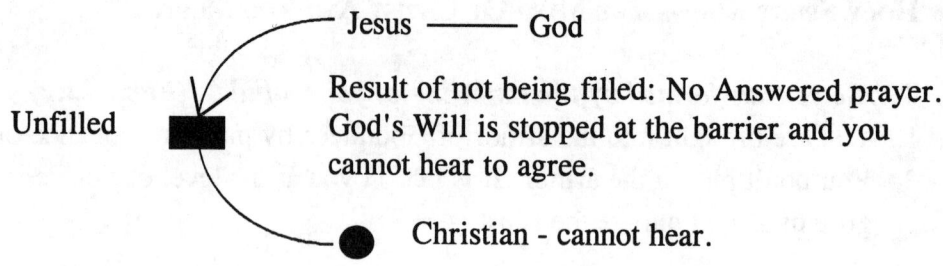

Jesus ——— God

Unfilled

Result of not being filled: No Answered prayer. God's Will is stopped at the barrier and you cannot hear to agree.

Christian - cannot hear.

E. Are you willing to pay any price to become a soldier of Christ?
   1. Forgive
   2. Financial responsibility
   3. Filled with the Holy Spirit *(John 16:13)*

F. Here are the procedures for the *"filling of the Spirit,"* **Ephesians 5:18**
   1. Have an overwhelming desire to Go on with God.
   2. Ask God to reveal you to you as He sees you.
      {True confession comes only when you, through conviction and contrition, (contrite heart means crushed over your sin *Isaiah 57:15, Isaiah 66:2),* confess in brokenness your deep sins, resulting in an overwhelming desire to be forgiven as the Holy Spirit reveals to you your sins, *(James 5:16).*}
   3. Then, ask God to fill you with His Spirit, believing that He will do it. Desiring His Lordship more than anything else in life will bring His transforming power to your being. But you must desire it above all things. That means...
      a. You will walk in the Spirit.
      b. You will live and work by the Spirit, *(Matt. 5:6).*

FURTHER THOUGHTS ON WALKING WITH GOD:

   1. God's ministry was through Jesus:
      Isa. 11:1-2, Isa. 42:1, Isa 61:1-3, , Matt. 3:11, 20:22-23, Luke 4:16-21, John 3:34, Acts 10:38, Gal. 3:14, Eph. 3:19

   2. Christ's Ministry is through us:
      Luke 24:49, John 7:37-38, John 14:12-15, Romans 15:28-29, Matt. 9:8, Acts 1:8, I Cor. 4:20, Eph. 3:20, I Thes. 1:5, II Thes. 1:11, II Peter 1:3.

   Q. What does it mean to be filled?
   A. The spirit empowers you for ministry.

TO BE FILLED:

   1. Take your life and pursue after Christ with all of your heart.
   2. When you are filled with Christ and begin to minister, He begins to empower you for ministry. He can penetrate the darkness.
   3. Present yourself a living sacrifice.
   4. Be transformed, not conformed, *Romans 12:1,2.*

Go Home...

1. Make sure you are saved.
2. Get Right / Forgive those who have spitefully used you, saved or lost. Leave those things behind.
3. Then, deal with your sin. Get right with your brother/sister in the Lord. Find out who you have hurt or harmed. Ask God if you are to go to them if you can't deal with it in prayer.
4. Allow God to order your finances.
5. Be willing to be filled and seek God for the filling of the Holy Spirit.
6. Ask Him to fill you and wait believing. He will do it if you desire Him with all of your heart. Fast if necessary; but wait, *Matthew 5:6.*
7. When it happens you will know it.

WHEN THOSE BARRIERS ARE BROKEN, PRAYER WORKS IN THIS WAY:

Step 1
God returns to you
with His Mind, Will, Kingdom,
Keys, etc...

Step 2
You agree

Step 3
God's Power moves in
to Answer.

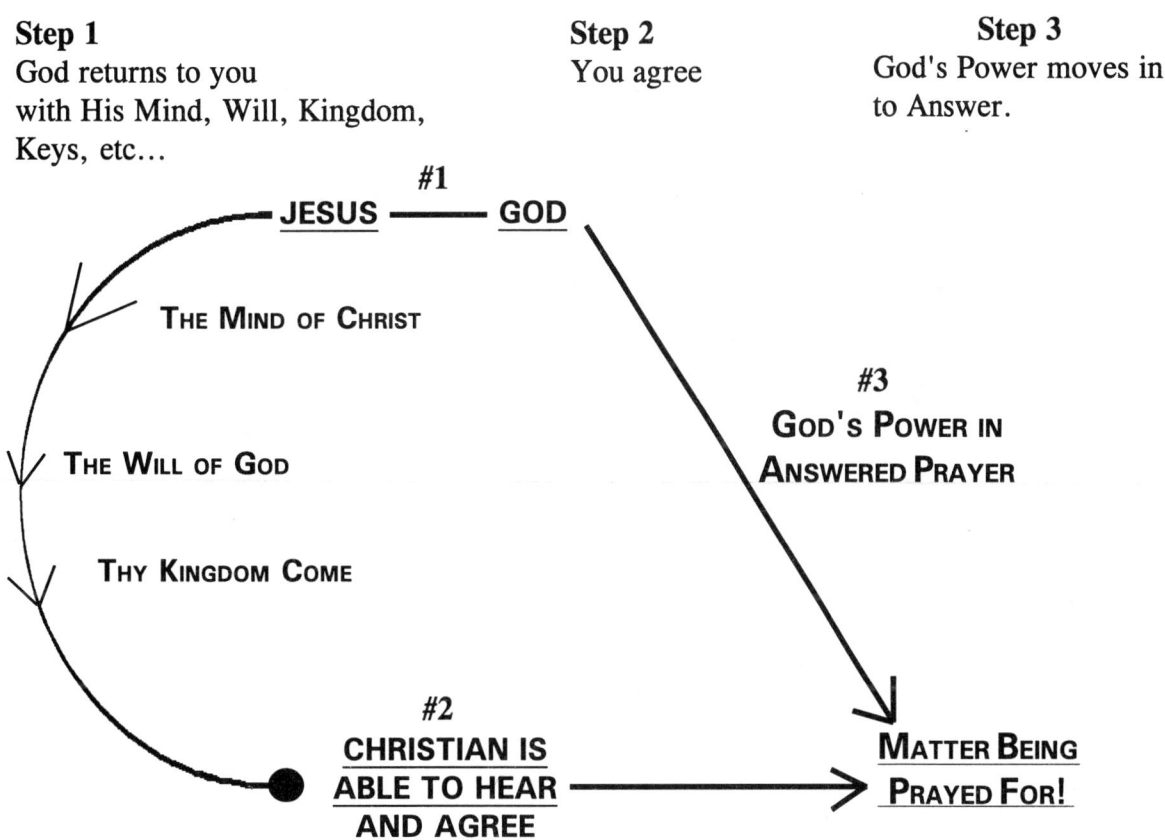

Again, you go to God in the Name of Jesus Christ. God returns His Will to your spiritual ear and hearing. You agree and God's Power moves in and satan is defeated.

"PRAYER: A WEAPON IN THE HANDS OF GOD"

SECTION SIX

The Power of Prayer and its availability to the Christian is so far beyond the mental grasp of the believer that it becomes impossible to comprehend. It would be like comprehending the total power of all the suns in all the galaxies and the pull of the stars in gravity. It would be like having the numbers to count all the particles of dust that make up all the planets in all the universes, known and unknown. It would be like explaining the Grace of God with adequate terms and words. It would take a billion lifetimes for the introduction to the subject matter. Such is prayer from God's side. Your side is to go in faith believing. God's side is supplying the Power at the level of your faith. This section will acquaint you first to what is available: the limitless power of God to increase your faith as you begin to comprehend in your spirit man. As the past is without date so is eternity. Herein lies the power of God through you, at the level of your faith.

Ephesians 1:16-22

16 *I cease not to give thanks for you, making mention of you in my prayers;*
17 *That the God of our Lord Jesus Christ, the Father of glory, may give unto you the spirit of wisdom and revelation in the knowledge of him:*
18 *The eyes of your understanding being enlightened; that ye may know what is the hope of his calling, and what the riches of the glory of his inheritance in the saints,*
19 *And what [is] the exceeding greatness of his power to us-ward who believe, according to the working of his mighty power,*

I. IN THESE VERSES WE SEE THE REAL POWER OF PRAYER WARFARE.

*Paul begins Warfare by attacking through Praise. *"I cease not to give thanks for you, making mention of you in my prayers."*

*In the Greek *verse 16* begins with *"I ... do not cease to give thanks for you, making mention of you in my prayers;"*

*What Paul is saying is that, "as I pray for you I give thanks"... (this is faith affirmed.)

    Q. How does God move into a matter through prayer?
    A. By Thanksgiving.

Thanksgiving is simply Faith Affirmation: your believing by faith that God has already begun to work. You begin to praise God in a matter as you pray. For you know by faith that God is going to do the work.

A. Thanksgiving moves God into a matter.
   1. Thanks is faith affirmation.
   2. Praise God in an issue as you begin to Pray.
   3. Praise is when, in prayer, you reach for God. High praise is God coming back through you to destroy satanic dominion in the area for which you are praying. Shout the victory before the battle! *(Joshua 6:5, Psalm 149:6, Psalm 22:3)*
   4. Again, you worship Him in the spirit by the spirit, *Phil 3:3 Amp*. High praise brings God's presence into the prayer.

B. "Look for a fight."
   1. All prayer is warfare. "War a good Warfare." "Watch ye therefore and pray," *I Timothy 1:18.*

C. Paul is doing warfare as he gives thanks for the church at Ephesus, *(verse 16).*

   16 (I) Cease not to give thanks for you, making mention of you in my prayers;

II. PAUL PRAYED THAT THE HOLY SPIRIT WOULD IMPRESS UPON THIS CHURCH WHO THEY WERE IN CHRIST, *(EPH. 1:17).*

   17 That the God of our Lord Jesus Christ, the Father of glory, may give unto you the spirit of wisdom and revelation in the knowledge of him:

A. Paul was praying in warfare as he sought God for these people.
   1. He began by praise, therefore disarming the enemy.
   2. Prayer warfare broke satan's ability to blind the minds as to who they were in Christ, *II Corinthians 4:3-4.*

B. Paul "knew God" in his spirit-man.
   1. You get to God through prayer.
   2. God gets to and through you by prayer.
   3. Answered prayer brings God through the believer at the level of His Will.
   4. Constant filling keeps the Spirit in control of your spirit-man.
   5. Again, prayer is not the position of the body but the condition of the heart.

C. To move to this level of praying the believer must cry out with Paul, *(Phil. 3:10):* *"That I may know him, and the power of his resurrection, and the fellowship of his sufferings, being made conformable unto his death..."*

   Again, the believer must ask God to break him, *(Isa. 57:15, 66:2).* He must be pursued.

D. Paul prayed for them to have *"knowledge"* of God.
   1. The Greek word "Knosis" is head knowledge. Carnal, baby, milk-fed Christians know that God answers prayer but He does not answer their prayer. They as babies can hear a voice but cannot understand it. They operate in religion or law.
   2. The Greek word "Epinosis" is higher knowledge, or revelation by the Holy Spirit that lives within. The will of God is given in prayer. The believer is maturing in Christ. Call, hear, understand, and agree.

3. God reveals Himself only through the Holy Spirit. All Christians have the Holy Spirit within and are therefore capable of discernment and direction, but they must by growth be able to understand.

4. Wisdom is knowing a thing works. Knowledge is the training in how to use it, such as owning a car before you learn to drive it.

5. The Holy Spirit builds you up in Holy faith, and brings to you the mind of the Spirit, such as *"Thy kingdom come, Thy will be done."* Revelation in prayer is being able to understand God's will and agree. Again, the word "effectual" in *James 5:16* means "God praying to God," or His *"Will be done."*

E. You Need...
   1. In *Eph. 1:17 That the God of our Lord Jesus Christ, the Father of glory, may give unto you the spirit of wisdom and revelation in the knowledge of him:*
      That the God of your Lord Jesus Christ, the Father of Glory may give unto ME the Spirit of Wisdom and Revelation in the Knowledge of Him.
      a. As you pray and seek God, He will through the Holy Ghost living within reveal the Spirit of Truth, (the Greek word for "Spirit" is "Pneuma").
      b. Wisdom that you know to pray, (Greek word "sophia" means "broad and full of intelligence").
      c. Revelation that you know what to pray for, (Greek word "apokalupsis" means "a disclosure of Truth").
      d. Knowledge of the involvement of His Will in the matter, that you can agree, (Greek word "gkepignosis" means "precise, and correct knowledge,") *(I John 4:17, Hebrews 5:14).*

F. *By having the eyes of MY heart flooded with Light, so that I can know and understand the hope of which He has called ME and how rich is His glorious inheritance in the saints - His set apart one. (Ephesians 1:18 Amp.)*
   1. When you begin to walk in the Spirit and God directs your life, you become sensitive to His voice and Will. Just as a child knows his earthly father's limitations, so you also become aware of God's inner-working for your life. Such is prayer, as God begins to open your eyes to His Will.
      a. "The Eyes of your understanding" means you know a thing in your spirit-man. The truth of faith is in *Hebrews 11:1.* Though you cannot see a thing, having prayed you know it to be so; therefore, it becomes substance, or that which you can hold on to. (Greek word "ophthalmos" meaning "the eyes of the mind, the faculty of knowing").
      b. "Understanding:" as you grow in the spirit, you discern more and more the voice of God in your inner man. Prayer is the activity of God through man, (Greek word "dianoid" meaning "the spirit way of thinking").
      c. "Enlightened:" you will see what God sees that you can agree, (Greek word "Photizo" meaning "bring to Light, make to see").
      d. "May know:" again, God reveals to your mind His Will to make substance, (Greek word "eido" meaning "to see - to behold").
      e. "Hope:" when you get a word from God in prayer you must get excited with joyful anticipation of the answer and victory. After all it is His Will you are agreeing with, (Greek word "elpis" meaning "hope, faith, expectation of good, joyful and confident expectation").
      f. "Calling:" to believe God at His word in prayer, (Greek word "lesis" meaning "to embrace").
      g. "Riches:" when you pray in God's Will you extract from His eternal kingdom's resources of which there is no limit, (Greek word "Ploutos" meaning "fullness, abundance").

h. "Inheritance:" all that God is, is given through man at the level of his faith, (Greek word "kleronomia" meaning "what is given to one as a possession, the eternal blessedness of the consummated kingdom of God").

i. "Saints:" You are pictured in this verse as holy and belonging to God, (Greek word "hagions" meaning "most holy thing, saint").

G. You find out who you are in Jesus by pursuing Him and having answered prayer.
  1. Force yourself to praise God through all tribulation, *(James 1:2-4 Amp.).*
  2. At that point your praise moves to high praise, (as God reaches down to you).
     Ps. 149:6-9, Isa. 61:1-3.
  3. Then you come alive to Jesus as He takes your cares and burdens upon Himself and makes a way of escape.
  4. God has pre-written the plan for your life through foreknowledge, beginning the day you were saved, *(Eph. 2:10 AMP).*

18 The eyes of your understanding being enlightened; that ye may know what is the hope of his calling, and what the riches of the glory of his inheritance in the saints...

⇒ Get your eyes on Jesus that you may be able to hear what His Will for you and through you is. You then become familiar with the riches that are in your "account" at the level of your faith. As your faith grows through answered prayer, you become more aware that your account can never be drained.

⇒ Begin to have answered prayer.

⇒ The riches and glorious inheritance is already in the life of the believer, *(Eph. 1:18).*

⇒ When you pray according to the Will of God, by the power of His name, God's inheritance is in your life, active and working. As your faith increases, you become more aware of an unlimited resource.

⇒ You are rewarded here and in heaven, not for what you do in the name of Jesus but what Christ is able to do through you in His name. Hearing, believing and praying, each time at a greater level.

III. AND WHAT [IS] THE EXCEEDING GREATNESS OF HIS POWER TO US-WARD WHO BELIEVE, ACCORDING TO THE WORKING OF HIS MIGHTY POWER? *(EPH. 1:19)*

19 And what is the exceeding greatness of his power to us-ward who believe, according to the working of his mighty power,

A. No other verse in the Bible uses these four words for the "power" that is available to the Christian at the level of his/her faith. Power: dunamis, working-energia, mighty-kratos, power - ischus

Verse 19 explains the use of this prayer power by giving two words:

  1. *"...exceeding..."* which is the Greek word "huperballo" meaning "far above measure, or beyond set limitation, transcend."
  2. *"...greatness..."* which is the Greek word "megethos" meaning "without bounds - considerable amount."

These are given to us!!!

B. The First Words Are...

"...of his power" this is the Greek word "Dunamis" or "Dynamo," which is a power source at the level of your faith in Christ, based on the activity of prayer and the practice of prayer. Your faith becomes stronger (without measure) each time you have answered prayer. The greater your ability to hear from God and agree, the more power is supplied through the practice of prayer by faith. As the Christian continues in faith praying, the more effectual he becomes. Therefore, through faith, God supplies a greater power, *(James 5:16)*.

THE BEST ILLUSTRATION OF THE WORD "DUNAMIS" IS "DYNAMO."

For example: If a light bulb had the capacity of 100 trillion watts, that is the amount of electricity that would illumine the bulb based on its current flow. Then if you designed a generator to reach this capacity, built it, put it on line, and began the process of sending a current through the lines, the light would begin to glow, but only at the level of power in flow.

The same is true with prayer. As you begin the practice of answered prayer, each experience of God's Glory, the dynamo, (or power source) becomes greater in your spirit. The dynamo in this case is faith. Your faith increases with each answer. Therefore, more power through the dynamo is emitted. In this case the power is unlimited as well as the light capacity. In other words, it is limited only to the level of your faith. As you continue to experience answered prayer you begin to live by the faith of the Son of God, *(Gal. 2:20)*.

C. *"...according to the working..."* which means "energeia," "display of power." You know when you pray that God is moving through you, *(Eph 3:7, 4:16, Phil 3:21, Col 1:29)*. "Energeia" is the word for energy.
   1. When the dynamo (power) supplies the electricity - energy - power for the bulb - the light comes on. (DISPLAY OF POWER)
   2. The bulb can take an unlimited amount of power.
   3. The source (God) is unlimited in power. Therefore, the amount of Light is only limited by the conduit or Christian's faith to bring Light or the Will of God into the matter.
   4. Satan operates in darkness. Christ is Light. So when you pray in faith believing, you bring Light into darkness thereby dispelling satanic demonic dominion.
   5. The key is believing: "*...the immeasurable and unlimited and surpassing greatness of His power in and for us who believe as demonstrated in the working of His Mighty strength,*" *(Eph. 1:19 AMP)*. What do you believe will happen when you pray? Better still, what does happen when you pray?

D. *"...mighty..."* is the Greek word "Ischus" - "force, ability, might, power, strength." (Jesus won at the cross.)

"Mighty" (v. 19) means "kratos" - "ruling power."

1. Satan's power was destroyed at the cross by the Blood of Jesus.
2. The name of Jesus destroys the work of the enemy as you use it in strength and force.
3. Another Greek term is Tharrheo. Its meaning is "to be bold, have confidence, be confident. "

E. *"...power..."* is the Greek word for "Kratos" which means "the King that is Ruling" or "dominion or might, power or strength."

This word for "power" means "the kingdom is already established." Satan was defeated the first time in heaven as Lucifer, and was cast here upon this Earth with the angels that followed him, *Isa. 14:9-7, Ezk. 28:11-19.*

He was stripped of power again at the cross by the Blood of Jesus Christ.

God wants to rule in every demonic circumstance, but He only rules through prayer.

1. The enemy fights prayer over everything else.
2. "Dead" churches (and individuals) have no power (Kratos) in their prayer lives.
3. The carnal Christian is no match for the wiles (methods) of the enemy, *Psalm 35:7, Ephesians 6:11.*

IV. WE HAVE RESURRECTION POWER (IN JESUS), AS GOD HAS SET HIM AT HIS OWN RIGHT HAND IN HEAVENLY PLACES, *(EPH. 1:20).*

> *20 Which he wrought in Christ, when he raised him from the dead, and set [him] at his own right hand in the heavenly [places].*

All the power that was described in *verse 19* was wrought or produced in Christ when God raised Him from the dead.

A. The word WROUGHT is the Greek word "energeo," which means to be "effectual, (fervent,) mighty in work." Effectual in prayer to Christ was God's power through Him at the level of His faith, which was pure faith. Real prayer to you is Christ through you in His will, (effectual means God praying to God,) or Christ in you the hope of glory.

B. When God RAISED Him from the dead He brought Him from inactivity to His Mighty Power. So are you when you present your body as a living sacrifice, *Rom. 12:1.* Then you have His mind, *Rom. 12:2.*

> *2 And be not conformed to this world: but be ye transformed by the renewing of your mind, that ye may prove what [is] that good, and acceptable, and perfect, will of God.*

Prayer is the mind of Christ through the heart of man at the level of his faith.

C. Such is the word "resurrected," which means "rise to life again, recovery of spiritual truth."

For example: If a person died and another picked up the body, the dead person's body would lathargically conform to the movements of the one carrying it. It would go where he carried it, in that it is dead having no fleshly functions. Such is the same with the Holy Spirit within you. You, at complete commitment and yielding of your will, have the Holy Spirit within you who develops through your spirit His Kingdom, His Will to be done on earth as it is in heaven.

D. Resurrection power is God's gift to Jesus Christ, given through you at the level of His will and your faith.

Q. What saved you?
A. The Resurrection.

Q. Where do you get your power?
A. The Resurrection.

Q. What do you have in you?
A. Resurrection Power! (The power that was wrought in Christ is in you.)

Q. Where is Christ?
A. The Right Hand of the Father.

Q. Where are you?
A. The Right Hand of the Father (seated with Christ in the heavenlies *Ephesians 2:6*).

Eph. 1:21 "Far above all principality, and power, and might, and dominion, and every name that is named, not only in this world, but also in that which is to come..."

A. Where is Christ and His Power? Far above all other power(s)!
1. Far above all principalities, order, or rank
2. Power: Authority, superhuman, token of control, (Greek Exousia).
3. Might: This is satan's power or jurisdiction, such as miraculous power or working of demonic miracles, (Greek dunamis).
4. Dominion: Mastery, Government. The idea is that nothing satan has established can even begin to stand against the resurrected power of Jesus Christ. All was conquered by His Blood and resurrection, (Greek, Kuriotes).
5. Name: No name written, known or unknown, can begin to rise against the Name of Jesus Christ, (Greek, onoma).
6. Not only in this world, "begin without end." Eternal, forever, world without end, (Greek Aion).
7. That which is to come would yet be.

B. How much more power does Jesus have than the enemy? All power! All authority!

Eph. 1:22 "And hath put all [things] under his feet, and gave him [to be] the head over all [things] to the church..."

C. Satan is "under Jesus' feet," *(Eph. 1:22).*
   1. You that are saved are the Church and have all authority in His Will to overcome the enemy. You are His body. Satan was totally defeated at the cross, by the Blood of Jesus Christ and His resurrection, (Greek "Aion").
   2. *And hath PUT under,* a place beneath, interior position. Through prayer in the application of the Blood, satan is then defeated at the level of your praying by faith, (Greek Hupdeigma).
   3. *Gave him to be the HEAD,* seizing the head, (Greek "Kephale").

Illustration: If you are going to seize a snake you do not grab it's tail, but rather its head. Such is the case of *Genesis 3:15, ("And I will put enmity between thee and the woman, and between thy seed and her seed; it shall bruise thy head, and thou shalt bruise his heel.")* Satan thought he had killed the Christ when he drove the nail through his heel. But that day, at the cross, the same heel came down on the head (Hebrosh) of satan and destroyed the power, and broke the fangs by His death, burial, and resurrection, *(I Cor. 2:7-8).* Such is the Power of Prayer.

   4. *Over all things to the CHURCH.* The *Church* is the community of saints on the earth.
   5. To every born again believer is given the power and privilege through prayer at the level of his faith, to destroy the works of the devil. This again is accomplished through the Blood and its application by the Holy Spirit through Prayer.

   Q. Where is satan?
   A. Under the Church / under your authority as a Christian through Christ.

To comprehend this power the Christian must learn of it through the practice of prayer. Its depth, height, and breadth is limited only by the faith of the believer. This section of the syllabus was shared as a glimpse of the Glory, "doxos," that is in us ready, to be used at the "Will of God." Prayer - practiced will bring participation of God's Will into your life. Without answered prayer you stand before Him in Judgment, *(II Cor. 5:10),* not having been used of Him. Study this chapter over and over. Become acquainted with who you are by finding out who He is and, who you represent. Ask for breaking. Receive it joyously. Deal with the areas in your life that are walls between you and your hearing from God. Truly come alive to the verse *"Learn of Me," (Matt. 11:29).* The yoke is wonderful. Prayer is God's Power through man.

PRAYER ASSAULT TEAMS

SECTION SEVEN

The remainder of this booklet provides a flow-chart and a step-by-step description of the overall structure of the Prayer Assault Teams.

Notice that the heading of Pastor is at the top of the flow-chart. If you are trying to implement this program in a church and you are not the Pastor, please do not utilize this method without explaining this program to your pastor. HIS COVERING IS NOT ONLY NECESSARY, BUT SCRIPTURAL.

Thank You,

MBEA

"CALLING AMERICA TO PRAYER"

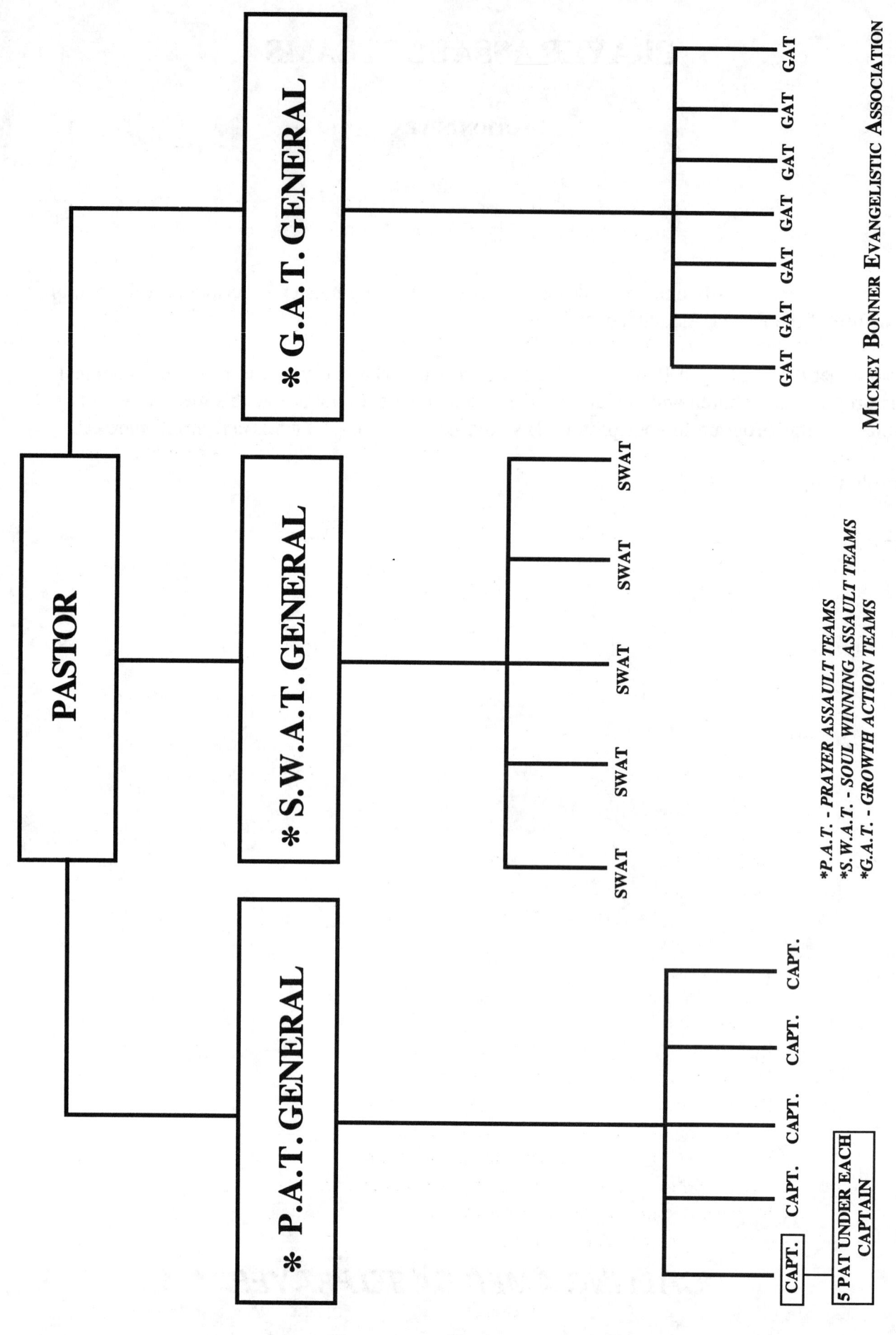

PASTOR

* P.A.T. GENERAL

* S.W.A.T. GENERAL

* G.A.T. GENERAL

CAPT. CAPT. CAPT. CAPT. CAPT.

SWAT SWAT SWAT SWAT SWAT

GAT GAT GAT GAT GAT GAT GAT

CAPT.

5 PAT UNDER EACH CAPTAIN

*P.A.T. - PRAYER ASSAULT TEAMS
*S.W.A.T. - SOUL WINNING ASSAULT TEAMS
*G.A.T. - GROWTH ACTION TEAMS

MICKEY BONNER EVANGELISTIC ASSOCIATION

74

P.A.T.

(PRAYER ASSAULT TEAMS)

PRAYER ASSAULT MINISTRY GUIDE

Welcome to spiritual warfare. We at MBEA want to congratulate you on your commitment to the Prayer Assault Ministry. It is our vision to develop prayer assault teams world wide. We are seeing wonderful results from prayer.

We realize your need for specific information to organize the Prayer Assault Ministry at your location. Our desire is to support your work and enable you to become as successful before the Lord as you can be.

To be successful in this prayer ministry there are a few "Nuts and Bolts" type suggestions we would like for you to consider. These are not mandatory but may be helpful to initiate your ministry more rapidly.

God bless you, and remember that "prayer brings God into the matter."

HOW PRAYER ASSAULT TEAMS ARE TO BE STRUCTURED

PERSONNEL:

(1) **PRAYER GENERALS:**

    (a)   Organize the local prayer assault ministry.
    (b)   Gather prayer requests (From - church members, friends, neighbors, Captains, Soldiers).
    (c)   Distribute prayer request to prayer Captains.
    (d)   Gather prayer victories and praise reports from Captains.
    (e)   Report prayer victories to church or organization.
    (f)   Are morale builder and trouble shooter for ministry.
    (g)   Supervise four or five Captains.

(2) **PRAYER CAPTAINS:**

    (a)   Receive prayer request(s) from General.
    (b)   Distribute prayer request(s) to Soldiers.
    (c)   Oversees the functioning of the prayer teams.
    (d)   Supervise not more than five prayer teams.
    (e)   Encourage and trouble shoots for prayer teams.
    (f)   Gather praise reports from teams and gives to General.
    (g)   Redistribute unanswered prayer to other teams if desired.
    (h)   Put your prayer teams together.

(3)   **PRAYER SOLDIERS:**

  (a)   Receive prayer requests from Captain.
  (b)   Pray with prayer partner daily or designated times.
  (c)   Pray for one or more requests a day.
  (d)   Pray five to ten minutes.
  (e)   Report all agreements, peace, or releases that God has answered to your prayer Captains.
  (f)   Pray and the other gives praise to God.
  (g)   If no agreement comes about the prayer request you may want to try again the next day. If still no agreement comes, give prayer request back to Captain to redistributed to another team.

PRAYER ASSAULT TEAMS SUGGESTIONS

PRAYER REQUESTS

The key to continued success in your prayer assault ministry will be your ability to maintain an extensive prayer request list. Your Soldiers will lose interest in the ministry without a constant supplying of prayer requests. Prayer Generals must be gathering and distributing prayer requests at all times.

PRAYER GENERAL'S PRAYER REQUEST FORM

Prayer #
Prayer Request:_____

_____

_____

Requested By: _____

Date: _____

Answer or distribution: _____

_____

_____

_____

REPORT AND PRAISE SESSION

A once-a-month prayer and praise session at the Church or in a General or Captain's home would be recommended. At this time you can share your ministries victories as well as needs. It would be a good time of fellowship and encouragement. This would be a good meeting to bring some prospective prayer soldiers to.

SCHEDULE OF EVENTS

DAILY   Monday thru Friday. Pray ten minutes a day with your prayer partner. Pray for one or more prayer request each day. Teams should be made up of: male/male; female/female; or husband/wife. You may even want to form youth teams. The prayer teams may want to pray over the phone or together in a home.

WEEKLY   On Mondays, Generals call Captains, and Captains call Soldiers to distribute or redistribute prayer requests. Captains should have called their teams before Monday to record the victories of answered prayers.

MONTHLY   Generals call a Report and Praise session at the Church or their home. Generals may want to prepare a Victory Letter of answered prayers to be mailed to all members of the Prayer Assault Ministry.

[Get right to praying! "Would you like to pray? I will give praise." After praying, if prayer partners are in agreement that their request has been answered, then they should report the victory to the prayer Captain. If release or agreement does not come then you may want to reschedule the request for the next day or give it back to your Captain for redistribution to another prayer team.]

PRAYER WARRIORS PREPARATION

(1)   Commit yourself to personal prayer and revival.
(2)   Surrender yourself to the Holy Spirit's control.
(3)   Thank God that your spiritual armor is in place in Christ Jesus. (helmet of salvation, breast plate of righteousness, belt of truth, sword of the Spirit, shield of faith, and prepared with the Gospel of peace).
(4)   Ask God to hedge you, your family, and your prayer partner about with His angels and hedge of thorns.
(5)   Ask God to rebuke Satan, his demons, and his servants away from you, your family, and your prayer partner spiritually, physically, emotionally, and mentally.
(6)   Confess all known sins in your life. (Ask God to reveal your sins to you and take time to listen).
(7)   Ask God to forgive you of your sins and accept His forgiveness. Then, forgive yourself.
(8)   Thank God for His forgiveness.
(9)   Thank God for answering all of your prayers.
(10)   Repeat the steps above as often as you feel you have sinned against God throughout the day.
(11)   Pray daily, preferably the first thing in the morning.

Remember - "Prayer is warfare and brings God into the matter. To function without prayer is to function without God. We go to God in the name of Jesus, bringing all that we believe about that name, holding it against the situation until it breaks."

S.W.A.T.

(Soul Winning Assault Teams)

It is imperative for the Prayer Assault Team General to put "feet" to the prayers that have been answered for salvation. These answered prayers must be followed up quickly. This will be done by S.W.A.T. teams, (Soul Winning Assault Teams). The following will be a step-by-step procedure for the Prayer Assault Team General or S.W.A.T. General to use. God will honor this method and many souls will be won to Christ and discipled for the glory of God.

Preparation and Deployment of S.W.A.T. Teams

(1)   The Pastor of a church or Prayer Assault Team General must be the coordinator who oversees the formulation of the S.W.A.T. team ministry. The P.A.T. General or Pastor should appoint a follow-through program. They also must gather from the P.A.T. as quickly as possible the names of those the teams have received a release or agreement on for salvation. These names must be distributed to the S.W.A.T. teams for visitation.

(2)   The S.W.A.T. Team General should be someone with a heart for evangelism. This person must be able to train the S.W.A.T. teams to evangelize. The General receives the names and addresses of those who have been prayed for and distributes them to their S.W.A.T. teams. Also the General will report back to the P.A.T. leader or Pastor the results of the visits.

(3)   S.W.A.T. teams are made up of born again believers who have a burden for lost souls. The teams will have either two men, two women, two youth of the same gender, or a married couple. They are to be trained in evangelism. They know that those whom they are visiting have been prayed through and are ready to receive their witness. Knowing this they will go in confidence and the power of the Holy Spirit. Where the P.A.T. teams have cultivated, the S.W.A.T. teams will reap.

(4)   Immediately following the visit the S.W.A.T. team will let the General know what happened in their meeting. They will also pass along what further actions are necessary. If someone accepted Christ Jesus as Lord of his life they need to be nurtured and discipled. He should be invited to church on Sunday and told that he can be given a ride to church. A time should be set up where you will follow up and begin to disciple the new Christian.

If the S.W.A.T. team was unable to reach the person then the visit should be rescheduled as soon as possible. If a person does not receive Christ during the visit his name needs to be given to the S.W.A.T. General and to the P.A.T. teams again for further prayer.

S.W.A.T. TRAINING

Once the S.W.A.T. teams have been organized the General needs to schedule the necessary evangelism training for the members. Thorough training will give your S.W.A.T. members that extra bit of confidence they will need. Success will come from a prepared and faithful soul winner.

A simple plan for leading someone to Christ has been used by Brother Bonner for many years and we suggest this method to you. The full soul winning plan can be found in a small booklet by C. S. Lovett. The title of the book is Soul Winning Is Easy. The S.W.A.T. General may want to purchase one to share with the S.W.A.T. members.

THE SOUL WINNING METHOD

THE APPROACH:

THREE QUESTIONS:

(1)   "Are You interested in spiritual things?" Regardless of his/her answer go ahead and ask the next question.

(2)   "Have you ever thought of becoming a Christian?" This question assumes that the person is not a Christian and forces them to reveal their relationship to Christ.

(3)   Suppose someone were to ask you, "What is a Christian?" What would you tell them? - After their response or responses you will give one of two answers:

   (a) If their answer is, "Someone who has made Jesus Christ their Lord and Savior." - Your response is, "Yes, have you had that experience?"

   (b) To most other responses you will reply, "Yes, that is what a Christian does but what is a Christian?"

THE GOSPEL

Ask permission to use the Word of God with them. Say, "With your permission I would like to read four verses of scripture and explain them to you. Then you will know what a Christian is." Quickly produce your tabbed New Testament and say, "God says that we are all sinners, as we see here in the Bible." **(Rom. 3:23)**

(1) *"For all have sinned and come short of the glory of God."*

You: "God tells us that we are all alike, we are all sinners. We know that is true don't we? For instance, have you ever told a lie?"

Them: "Sure, who hasn't?"

You: "We all have. Well then, how many lies does it take to make you a liar?" (hold one finger out)

Them: "Just one I suppose."

You: "So how many sins do you suppose it would take to make us a sinner?"

Them: "One"

You: "If Jesus Christ were standing right here next to you would you say that you are more righteous than He?"

Them: "No"

You: "Why not?"

Them: "I'm just not."

You: "That is right. It said that in this scripture, "*For all have sinned and come short of the glory of God.*"

(Quickly turn to the next scripture - **Rom. 6:23a**)

(2) *"The wages of sin is death...*

You: "If you or I work for our employer for a whole week we expect to get paid a weeks wages, don't we?"

Them: "I do."

You: "God says, *'The wages of sin is death'*, and you can expect to be paid for your sin. Some one has to pay for them. This death is an eternal separation from God."

You: "But now let's hear what God has to say when He no longer is talking about death but life everlasting as a gift." **(Rom. 6:23b)**
"*...The gift of God is eternal life through Jesus Christ our Lord.*"

"The eternal life God has to offer is a free gift. You can't earn a gift or pay for a gift can you?"

Them: "No."

You: "A gift can only be received or rejected. God is offering you eternal life as a free gift right now. Let's imagine this blank card is a five dollar bill. I want to give this card to you as a gift, but I put it into the Bible first and hand it to you. You would take the Bible to get the five dollar bill wouldn't you?

"The gift of eternal life God is offering you is also in someone, His Son Jesus Christ."

"Remember, the gift is a free gift. It is the gift of eternal life and it is in Christ Jesus. We must take Christ in order to get it." **(John 1:12)**

> **(3)** *"But as many as "received" Him, to them gave He power to become the sons of God, "*

You: "Many people believe a lot about Jesus Christ but just believing is not enough to get you eternal life. God wants you to receive Jesus into your life."

"Let me illustrate. I offer this card to you as a free gift. You believe me don't you."

Them: "Yes, I believe you."

You: "But you don't have it, do you?" Why not?"

As long as the card is in my hand it doesn't matter how much you believe. You still don't have it, do you?"

Them: "No."

You: "In the same way each of us must receive Christ. Just as you had to take the card to get it you also must take Christ as your Savior to receive the free gift of eternal life. Here is how to do it."

"Jesus is saying," **(Rev. 3:20)**

> **(4)** *"Behold I stand at the door, and knock: If any man hear my voice, and open the door, I will come in to him."*

You: "The Lord says that He is standing at the door of your heart. The Lord will not force His way into your life. You have a free will and must invite Christ into your life. He is waiting to come in to your life."

"If I was a good friend of yours and came to your house and knocked on the door, what would you say?"

Them: "I would say come in."

You: "Jesus is waiting to come into your heart. Would you ask Him to come in?"

"Bow your head with me. Just tell the Lord that you know you are a sinner and you want Him to forgive you. Ask Him to come into your life and save you. Can you do that?"

Them: The response may be, "I don't know how."

You: "I will help you. Please pray after me."

INVITATIONAL PRAYER: "Lord I'm a sinner. I ask you to forgive me of my sin. I ask you to come into my life and be my Lord and Savior. Make my life the way you want it to be. Thank you for saving me."

You: "Did you mean what you just prayed?"

Them: "Yes"

You: "Then according to the scripture I just read to you, where is Christ Jesus right now in relation to you?"

Them: "In my life."

You: "Congratulations"

"May I come by this Sunday morning and take you to church with me?"

G.A.T.

(Growth Action Teams)

In order to complete the cycle of ministry to these new Christians we must follow up our prayer and evangelism with some tender love and care. We must not allow these baby Christians to slip through the cracks of indifference or neglect. The Growth Action Teams will specifically address this important need. We have experienced, in many instances, that new Christians don't receive adequate follow up and don't grow spiritually. They remain babes in Christ. The Growth Action Teams will nurture the new Christian. Here is the structure and process.

(1) G.A.T. GENERAL:

(a) This person will be chosen by the Pastor and could be a staff member.

(b) They will oversee the Growth Action Teams and Coordinate their ministry.

(c) The General will first train the G.A.T. workers for their special task of love.

(d) The General will report to the pastor the progress of the new Christian.

(e) The G.A.T. General and the S.W.A.T. General must by necessity work closely together. The spiritual growth of the new converts depend on it.

(f) The G.A.T. General will make all assignments to the G.A.T. and will direct them in the amount of time spent with each new Christian.

(g) They will also receive from G.A.T. prayer requests concerning the new Christians.

(2) G.A.T. WORKERS:

(a) These teams will be selected by the Pastor or G.A.T. General. Because of the nature of the ministry it would be ideal if these teams were comprised of Families in the church.

(b) They will receive orientation and ministry training from their G.A.T. General.

(c) They will receive assignments from their G.A.T. General.

(d) The G.A.T. Worker will be assigned to the new Christian for a period of six to eight weeks or until the G.A.T. General releases them.

(1) They will provide Friendship to the new Christian in the church and make them feel at home and loved.

(2) They are to offer Fellowship to the new Christian by inviting them over to their home for fellowship with other Christians. They will accompany them to other church sponsored fellowships.

(3) They must Follow-Up with this new Christian to bring them to church; try to enroll them in Sunday School; encourage them to be baptized and join the church; promote their spiritual growth by teaching them aggressive warfare praying before they teach them doctrine.

(4) The G.A.T. will report weekly to the G.A.T. General about the progress of their new Christian.

"MAY GOD CONTINUALLY BLESS YOU IN THIS EXCITING MINISTRY."

BASIC CELL GROUP SEMINAR

I. MINISTRY OF THE CHURCH

(A) Temple ministry
(1) Preaching
(2) Teaching
(3) Worshipping

(B) House to house ministry *(Acts 2:46-47)*
(1) Christian ministry
(2) Early church ministry in homes
    (a) Lydia's, *(Acts 16:40)*
    (b) Aquila and Priscilla's, *(Rom. 16:3-5)*
    (c) Philemon's, *(Philemon 2)*

(C) Delegation of authority
(1) Pastor to Elders -- Moses *(Exod. 18:21-22)*
(2) Elders to People -- *(2 Tim. 2:2)*
(3) People to people -- *(Heb. 10:24-25, 2 Tim. 2:24-25, 1 Pet. 4:10, Col. 1:28-29, 2 Tim. 2:2)*

(D) Pastor free to pray and minister God's Word

II. CELL GROUP LEADERSHIP

(A) Pastor:
(1) Oversees total church ministry.
(2) Teaches weekly training session to Cell Group Leaders.
    (a) Teaches Bible lesson to be taught in Cell Group.
    (b) Answers questions Cell Group Leaders have.
    (c) Receives reports from Elders.

(B) Elder or Deacon:
(1) Area Directors.
(2) Report to Pastor.
(3) Could possibly be a Cell Group Leader.
(4) Receives reports from Cell Group Leaders.

(C) Cell Group Leader:
(1) Has an evangelistic zeal, *(2 Cor. 5:19-21, Matt. 28:19-20, 4:19, John 20:21).*
(2) Leads Cell Group meetings.
(3) Reports all necessary information to Elder.
(4) Trains Assistant Cell Group Leader.
(5) This person may be a man or woman.

(D) Assistant Cell Group Leader:
(1) Responsible to Cell Group Leader.
(2) In training for six months.
(3) Becomes new Cell Group Leader when Cell multiplies.

III.   STEPS TO ORGANIZING THE CELL GROUP MINISTRY

(1)   Pastor shares Cell Group Concept with church.
(2)   Choose your leadership.
(3)   Leadership is trained.
(4)   Choose your target areas of ministry for Pilot Cell Groups.
(5)   Cell Leaders form their groups from members in their area.
(6)   Give member all relevant information about their group.
(7)   Limit size of Cell groups to 15 families.
(8)   Make sure two-way lines of communications between all of leadership are kept open and are functioning.
(9)   Keep good statistics -- attendance, salvations, answered prayer.
(10)   Nurture those first groups for 6 to 8 months.
(11)   Take plan to whole church and get as many involved as possible. You may want to have sign-up lists available or just assign members to a Cell Group.

IV.   WEEKLY CELL GROUP MEETINGS

(1)   Rotate to be in a different members home each week.
(2)   Cell Group Leader in charge of each meeting.
(3)   Meeting should last about an hour and a half.
(4)   Meeting opens by recognizing visitors.
(5)   Leader "icebreaker" question for all to answer.
(6)   Praise Leader sings, accompanied by guitar or tapes.
(7)   Prayers and testimonies of praise should be spontaneous at this time.
(8)   Leader teaches Bible lesson and leads in discussion.
(9)   Members share prayer requests and minister to each other through prayer and discussion.
(10)   Evangelism is always to be encouraged in the groups. The members should be encouraged to bring a neighbor or friend to the next meeting.
(11)   Plan monthly socials, where several Cell Groups can come together for fun and fellowship.